PEDAGOGY OF SCHOOL SUBJECT CHEMISTRY

(Volume – I)

Dr. Yadukumar M

Title of the book:
Pedagogy of School Subject Chemistry

Author:
Dr. Yadukumar M
Assistant Professor
Kumadvathi College of Education
Shikaripura

First Edition:
August, 2024

Price:

ISBN:

Published by:
Notion Press Media Pvt Ltd,
#7, Red Cross Road,
Egmore, Chennai, Tamil Nadu 600008
Email ID: publish@notionpress.com
Phone Number: +91 44 46315631

Contents

UNIT I - Nature, scope, objectives and values of chemistry

1-42

1.1 Meaning and nature of chemistry

1.2 Scope of teaching chemistry with special reference to Agriculture, Industry and Medicine.

1.3 Contribution of Indian scientists in the field of chemistry.

1.4 General Objectives of teaching Chemistry

1.5 Instructional Objectives: Knowledge, understanding, application, skill, attitudes and appreciation.

1.6 Values of teaching Chemistry- Intellectual, utilitarian, disciplinary, vocational and cultural.

1.7 Relating objectives with content units of secondary schools.

UNIT II- Planning for teaching chemical science

43-88

2.1 Lesson Plan: Meaning, importance, steps and format

2.2 Planning and use of ICT and 5E lesson plan

2.3 Unit Plan: Meaning, importance, components and steps

2.4 Resource Unit: Meaning, Components, Steps and Importance.

2.5 Chemistry laboratory: importance, designing, planning, equipping, maintenance of biological equipment and records.

Preface

Chemistry education is the study of teaching and learning chemistry. Topics in chemistry education include understanding how students learn chemistry and determining the most efficient methods to teach chemistry. There is a constant need to improve chemistry curricula and learning outcomes. Chemistry education can be improved by changing teaching methods and providing appropriate training to chemistry teachers, within many modes, including classroom lectures, demonstrations and laboratory activities.

This book titled by Pedagogy of school subject chemistry (Volume-I) gives information about the teaching and learning process of Chemistry. It covers whole syllabus of Pedagogy of school subject chemistry for second semester B.Ed Student Teachers of Kuvempu University. This book not only limited to Kuvempu University student Teachers, but it also helps to other Indian Universities.

Dr. Yadukumar M

Date:30-08-2024

Acknowledgments

Little drops of water make the mighty ocean. As such, every year my student teachers are happy to learn and encourage me to teach with innovative teaching methods. I was able to publish this book with the inspiration of our previous batch Student Teachers. So this book is completely dedicated to the previous batch Student Teachers of our college.

I extend my sincere gratitude to my students, whose enthusiasm and curiosity have fueled my passion for teaching. Finally, I dedicate this book to the countless learners who seek knowledge and inspirations. May this book serve as a catalyst for their professional growth and life long learning.

Unit I - Nature, scope, objectives and values of Chemistry

1.1 Meaning and nature of chemistry

Meaning of Chemistry

Chemistry is the branch of science that deals with the composition and properties of substances and various elementary forms of matter.

Chemistry is the systematic study of the properties and structure of the chemical elements and their compounds.

Chemistry is the systematic study of the preparation, properties, structure and reactions of the chemical elements and their compounds and of the systems which they form.

The study of the elements and the compounds they form and action one upon other.
- Oxford Chemistry

Chemistry is the integrated study of the nature, structure, properties and reactions of the chemicals, elements and their properties.
- Ragunathana K. V

Chemistry is the integrated study of the nature, structure, properties and reactions of the chemical elements and their compounds and systems which they form.
- M S Yadav

Chemistry is the science of molecular behavior.

Nature of chemistry

- Chemistry is the study of the composition, structure, and properties of matter and of changes (transformations) that occur in matter.

- Matter is the building block material of the universe. It is anything that takes up space and has mass.

Chemistry is a basic science whose central concerns are:

1. Structure and behaviour of atoms.

2. Composition and properties of compounds.

3. Reactions between substances with their accompanying energy exchange; and

4. The laws that unite these phenomena into a comprehensive system.

1.2 Scope of teaching chemistry with special reference to Agriculture, Industry and Medicine

Chemistry is important in everyday

Everything is made of chemicals. Example: Fuels, Food, Fibres, Dyes, Drugs, Animal husbandry, Health, Industries, Agriculture. Many of the changes we observe in the world around us are caused by chemical reactions. Examples include leaves changing colors, cooking food and getting you clean.

The scope of chemistry in Agriculture

- ➢ The basic need of human being is food.

- ➢ It is the agriculture only which fulfills this need for the entire population of the world.

- ➢ Plants are called producers as they synthesize their own food using CO_2 from air and water from soil utilizing sunlight as source of energy by a process known as photosynthesis.

- ➢ The rest of the food chain consists of consumers only.

- ➢ The practice of producing crops and livestock from the natural resources of the earth is called Agriculture.

- ➢ Modern agriculture includes agronomy, horticulture, animal husbandry, dairying, soil chemistry, etc.

- ➢ Chemistry deals with compounds, both organic and inorganic.

- ➢ Agriculture deals with the production of organic products using both organic and inorganic inputs.

> Thus Chemistry forms an integral part of agriculture from molecular to organ level. It plays a role from the basics of photosynthesis to the utilization of agricultural produce.

Role of Chemistry in agriculture

Photosynthesis: This natural process provides the basic building block for all the agricultural products. The overall process is best shown by the net equation.

$$6CO_2 + 6H_2O ==> C_6H_{12}O_6 + 6O_2$$

Without photosynthesis, not only would there be no plants, the planet could not sustain life of any kind.

1. Fertilizers:

Fertilizer is any organic or inorganic material of natural or synthetic origin that is added to a soil to supply one or more plant nutrients essential to the growth of plants.

Fertilizers can be divided into two categories

> Organic fertilizers

> Inorganic fertilizers

Organic fertilizers are derived from living systems and include animal manure, fish and bone meal, and compost. These organic fertilizers are decomposed by microorganisms in the soil to release their nutrients for use by plants.

Chemical fertilizers are less complex and have high concentrations of chemicals that may be in short supply in the soil namely nitrogen, phosphorous, potassium, calcium, magnesium and sulfur. Fertilizers also provide micro nutrients which are required in much smaller quantities namely boron, chloride, copper, iron, manganese, molybdenum and zinc.

Inorganic fertilizer is synthesized using the Haber-Bosch process, which produces ammonia as the end product. This ammonia is used for other nitrogen fertilizers, such as anhydrous ammonium nitrate and urea. Now fertilizers with slow release of nutrients have been developed.

Appropriate use of fertilizers to increase crop yield has counterbalanced loss of land due to urbanization and significantly supported global population growth, It has been estimated that almost half the people on the Earth are currently fed as a result of synthetic nitrogen fertilizer use.

2. Pesticides and Insecticides

In order to minimize the damage of the crops by pests a large variety of chemicals known as pesticides are used. Subclasses of this are herbicides, insecticides, fungicides, rodenticides and biocides depending on its target.

Insecticides are chemicals that are used to kill insect because they can spread livestock diseases, can eat stored grain, and can feed on growing crops. However not all insects are harmful and certain species of insects are needed to pollinate plants to ensure that they set seed.

3. Storage and preservation of agriculture produce:

Sulfur dioxide is used to keep grain fresh and useable for a longer period of time. Food preservatives like sodium benzoate and salicylic acid are used for longer shelf life. New generation refrigerants have been developed. Chemicals are added to promote the ripening of fruits or the germination of seeds. Food packaging has advanced due to the material produced by advancements in chemistry. Agricultural chemistry has increased the diversity of the human diet and has led to a greater overall availability of food, both animal and plant.

4. Food Processing:

Development of saccharin and other sweeteners, vitamins and minerals, consumers have benefited from new technologies that have enhanced the flavor, appearance, availability, and nutritional value of their food.

5. Chemicals from agriculture waste:

Advancement in Chemistry has resulted in development of technologies to produce a variety of chemicals from agricultural waste. Production of alcohol from bagasse which is used as the feedstock for chemicals is good example.

6. Chemistry in other areas of agriculture:

Plastic pipes for improved irrigation: Plastic was derived from chemistry and this is widely used in agriculture. This has increased irrigation massively which results in a better environment for the crops to prosper in.

The Scope of Chemistry in Industry

Chemistry plays an important and useful role towards the development and growth of a number of industries. This includes industries like glass, cement, paper, textile, leather, dye etc. We also see huge applications of chemistry in industries like paints, pigments, petroleum, sugar, plastics, Pharmaceuticals.

It has also helped in the greater production of sulphuric acid, nitric acid, and Ammonia, hydrogenated oils by providing suitable catalysts.

1. Food Industry

Chemicals play a major role in our food. The preservatives, taste enhancers and flavors helps the food to be palatable and increase the shelf life. Food Industry thrives for the reason, that the preservatives not only help them to maintain the quality of the food, but also helps them to import food to different parts of the world. Due to these advancements, we are able to enjoy fruits, canned food products, and ready-to-eat food products across the world. More than 80% of the chemical industry concentrates on producing Polymers and Plastics. They are not only used in packing but also in numerous other things like wiring, furniture, clothing, home décor, prosthesis and electronics. PVC piping, water tanks, huge storage containers are made out of plastics.

Fertilizers and pesticides aids in the agriculture and development. The green revolution has happened only due to the advancement of chemical industry in India. The fertilizers and pesticides, not only increase the yield of the crop, but prevent from pest attacks.

Apart from in-house usage of food products within our country, we are also exporting a lot of grains, fruits, flowers and ornamental stem to various parts of the world. The GDP of the country drastically increases with the industry.

2. Pharmacy industries

Pharma industries and lifesaving drugs are the fastest growing industry in India. Our country invites a lot of people for medical tour. Numerous laboratories are also set-up to study various drug for the endemic and epidemic diseases. Before these laboratories in our country, we have been exporting a lot of chemicals, which was expensive and mostly unaffordable for a large sector of people.

3. Colorants:

- You may be familiar with dyes and pigments used in such things as industries like textile, paints and ceramics.

- Pigments are insoluble compounds, meaning they are colourful particules that do not fully dissolve.

- Think of it like muddy water, you can and mix dirt and water together to make a muddy brown colour, but if you let the water sit, all the particles separate and sink to the bottom of the cup.

- Dyes, on the other hand, are soluble compounds, which they dissolve in water.

4. Fuels:

- Any chemical with stored energy is referred to as a fuel.

- Photosynthesis and respiration are two processes that store this energy in chemical bonds in the molecules.

- During oxidation, energy is released. The prevalent type of oxidation is the combustion. This is the direct reaction of a fuel with oxygen.

5. Wars:

- Gunpowder's used in bullets. Other explosives used in wars are all chemical compounds.

- Nuclear weapons which have become more well known in recent years are also chemical compounds.

6. Textiles:

- Textile may undergo a variety of chemical and non-chemical treatments during the manufacturing process , including preparation and pre-treatment, dyeing, printing and fabric refining.

- Textiles and clothing contain a wide range of chemicals. Some are used to provide a product with a specific effect.

- Such as biocides to prevent mould from forming on shoe, dyes to give clothing their distinct colours and water repellents to make outdoor wear more practical.

7. Soaps and cleaners:

- Soaps are made from natural animal fats and vegetable oils that go through a process called saponification.

- Soaps are one type of cleaner, but there are many other types that use different ingredients and processes for different applications in which dirt needs to be removed.

- Without the chemistry involved to make specific soaps and cleaners.

- We would not have products such as body gels, fabric softeners, laundry detergents.

- Synthetic sulphates have allowed us to utilize a new generation of gentler cleaning products for our bodies and homes.

The scope of chemistry in Medicine

Many substances from natural sources have been used since times immemorial for treatment of diseases. At present we can isolate and purify the drug from natural sources and establish their chemical structure. Sparsely occurring substances can be synthesized in the laboratory and in this way made available in abundance. Even such drugs which do not occur in nature have also been obtained by synthesising them in the laboratory.

Analgesics: The substances which relieve pain are called analgesic.

Antipyretics: The substances which are used to bring down the body temperature in high fever are called antipyretics. Ex: Aspirin, Paracetomol, Analgin, Novalgen etc.

Antibiotics: The chemical substance produced or derived from the micro organisms which are capable of destroying the micro organisms are called antibiotics. Ex Penicillin, Ampicillin, Streptomycin etc.

Tranquilizers: The substances which produce soothing affect on mind are called tranquilizers.

Antimalarial: These are drugs used in the treatment of malaria. Ex: Chloroquin, quinine, plasmoquin

Antiseptics: The chemical substance which prevent the growth of micro organisms or destroy them but are not harmful to the living human tissues are called antiseptics.

1.3 Contribution of Indian scientists in the field of chemistry

Acharya Kanad

- He was the founder of Vaisheshik Darsham

- He is believed to have been born in Prabhas Kshetra near Dwarika in Guja rat.

- He has classified all the objects of creation Into nine elements namely Earth, Water, Light, Wind, Sky Time, Space, Mind and Soul

- He says every object of creation is made of atoms which in turn connect with each other to form molecule s.

- He also described the dimension and motion of atoms and their chemical reactions with each other

- T, N colebrok Has said Compared to the scientists of Europe, kanad and other Indian scientists were the global masters of this field

Nagarjuna

- He was an extraordinary wizard of science Born in the village of Baluka in Madhya Pradesh

- Textual masterpieces like "Ras Ratnakar, "Rashrndaya", "Rase ndramangal", are his renowned contributions to the science of chemistry

- He discovered the alchemy of transmitting bone metals into gold

- He was the author of medical books like Arogyamanjari and Yogasar he also made significant contribution to the field of curative medicine

- He was appointed as chancellor of the famous University of Nalanda Nagarjuna's milestone discoveries impress and astomish the scientists of today

Animesh Chakravorty

Animesh Chakraborty is a Bengali Indian academic and a professor of che mistry. In 1975, he was awarded the Shanti Swarup Bhatnagar Prize for Science and Technology in chemistry by the Council of Scientific and Industrial Research.

Age: 82

Birthplace: Kolkata, India

C. N. R. Rao

Chintamani Nagesa Ramachandra Rao FRS, also known as C.N.R. Rao, is an Indian chemist who has worked mainly in solid-state and structural chemistry. He currently serves as the Head of the Scientific Advisory Council to the Prime Minister of India. Rao has honorary doctorates from 60 universities from around the world. He has authored

around 1,500 research papers and 45 scientific books. On 16 November 2013, the Government of India announced his selection for Bharat Ratna, the highest civilian award in India, making him the third scientist after C.V. Raman and A. P. J. Abdul Kalam to receive the award.

Age: 83

Birthplace: Bangalore, India

Debashis Mukherjee

Debashis Mukherjee is one of the pioneers of Modern Theoretical Chemistry, well known for his research in the fields of molecular many body theory, theoretical spectroscopy, finite temperature non-perturbative many body theories. Mukherjee has been the first to develop and implement a

class of many-body methods for electronic structure which are now standard works in the field. These methods, collectively called multireference coupled cluster formalisms, are versatile and powerful methods for predicting with quantitative accuracy the energetics and cross-sections of a vast range of molecular excitations and ionization.

Age: 71

Birthplace: Naihati, India

Garikapati Narahari Sastry

Garikapati Narahari Sastry is an Indian chemist. He heads the Molecular Modeling Division at the Indian Institute of Chemical Technology in Hyderabad, India. Sastry has made pioneeing contributions in the areas of computational chem istry and computational biology. He was awarded Shanti Swarup Bhatnagar Prize for Science and Technology in 2011, the highest science award in India, in the chemical sciences category.

Age: 52

Birthplace: Andhra Pradesh, India

Gautam Radhakrishna Desiraju

Gautam Desiraju has played a major role in the development of crystal engineering for nearly three decades. He, among others, has been re sponsible in recent times for the acceptance of the theme of weak hydrogen bonding in structural and supramolecular chemistry. His books on crystal engineering and on the weak hydrogen bond in structural chemistry and

biology are especially notable. He has co-authored a textbook in crystal engineering. He is one of the most highly cited Indian chemists and has been recognised by a number of awards such as the Alexander von Humboldt Forschungspreis and the TWAS award in Chemistry.

Age: 65

Birthplace: Chennai, India

Govindarajan Padmanabhan

Govindarajan Padmanaban is an Indian biochemist and biotechnologist. He was the former director of the Indian Institute of Science, and presently serves as honorary professor in the department of biochemistry.

Age: 80

Birthplace: Chennai, India

Prafulla Chandra Ray

Acharya Prafulla Chandra Ray was a Bengali chemist, educator and entrepreneur. The Royal Society of Chemistry honoured his life and work with the first ever Chemical Landmark Plaque outside Europe. He was the founder of Bengal Chemicals &  Pharmaceuticals, India's first pharmaceutical company. He is the author of A History of Hindu Chemistry from the Earliest Times to the Middle of Sixteenth Century.

Age: Died at 83 (1861-1944)

Birthplace: Khulna, Bangladesh

Ramanbhai B Patel

- He was born On 19 August 1925 - 19 September 2001

- Patel was Born at kathar in south Gujarat and studied chemistry at Gujarat University LM College of pharmacy 

- The production Of Isopal a formulation of the antituberculosis drugs isoniazid and para amino salicylic acid in 1957

- Neuronin -12 a single vial mixture of vitamin B1 , vitamin B6 and vitamin B 12 in 1959

- In 1973 the firm developed process technology to make the antidiabetic drug glibenclamide

- In 1971 the firm launched Dexona – 20 which was a concentrated form of the anti inflammatory drug dexamethasone

1.4 General Objectives of teaching Chemistry

Educational objectives

Educational objectives may be defined as a desired change in behavior in a person that we are trying to bring about through education.   **– E. J Frust.**

An educational objective can be defined as a desired change in the behavior of individuals through the Education.

OBJECTIVES OF TEACHING SCIENCE

Education is a process of bringing about changes in an individual in a desired direction. It is a process of helping a child to develop his potentialities to the maximum and to bring out the best from within the child. To bring about these changes we teach them various subjects at different levels of school. Science as subject is included in the school curriculum from the very beginning.

Importance of Educational objectives

- It provides the direction to the activity which is designed for achieving an ultimate goal.

- It provides the basis for organizing activities.

- The possible achievement in terms of what the students is able to do, when the whole education system is directed towards Educational Aims.

- Determine the nature of Educational activities.

- Provide direction to these activities both in curricular and co-curricular areas.

- Priorities activities in an educational process.

- Provide a basis for developing a curriculum hence text books, workbooks and teacher guides.

- Evolve a basis for development of skills and abilities in learners and their evaluation.

- Promote moral and spiritual values.

- Identify the strengths and weaknesses of pupils learning as well as that of the system.

- Educational objectives have a role to play both from teaching as well as testing point of view.

- The Educational objectives are broad and they are related to educational system and school.

- The Educational objectives may be achieved by organizing teaching from primary to university level.

- Educational objectives are to develop the feeling of national integration.

- Educational objectives can be helpful in Instructional planning during the teaching – learning process and when assessing student progress.

Types of Objectives

- General objectives of teaching Chemistry

- Specific objectives of Chemistry

General objectives of teaching chemistry

- To make students interested in chemistry

- To familiarise the students with the important role played by chemistry in their life.

- To develop scientific culture in students.

- To provide a training to students in methods of science.

- To emphasise upon students the role of chemistry on social behaviour.

- To prepare students for those vocations which require a sound knowledge of chemistry.

- To increase students understanding to such a level that he can understand various concepts and theories that unifies various branches of chemistry.

1.5 Instructional Objectives

The specific objectives under cognitive, affective and psychomotor domain are clubbed into three, two and one respectively for the purpose of formulating general instructional objectives for science teaching. These are as follows.

- Knowledge

- Understanding and

- Application arc from the cognitive domain,

- Interest and

- Attitude are from the affective domain and

- Skill is Prom thc psychomotor domain.

By now you are familiar with these terms. Let us now discuss these objectives as they are used for instruction purpose along with expected change in behaviour of learners.

Knowledge

Knowledge as you know is the lowest level of cognitive ability. Therefore, the first objective of teaching science is related to acquisition of knowledge by the students. It states: "Students will   acquire the knowledge of facts, concepts, principles, processes and techniques etc."

The behaviour specification to demonstrate the achievement of this objective is that pupil will be able to:

- *Recall* terms, facts, concepts, principles and processes etc.

- *Recognize* facts, terms, concepts, principles and processes etc.

You know that words like 'recall' and 'recognize' are the action words which represent the behaviour of individuals. This overt behaviour can be observed and measured by teacher as well as by an evaluator or any observer.

Comprehension or Understanding

The second objective of science teaching is related to the next higher cognitive ability i.e. comprehension or understanding.

It states: "To develop the ability to understand facts, concepts, principles, theories and techniques etc."

Behaviour specifications of objectives are that pupils:

- *Illustrate* terms, facts, concepts, principles etc. by citing examples.

- *Express* the same fact or concept in different ways by way of explanation.

- *Locate* errors in known situation and correct them.

- *Compare* and contrast between related terms and concepts.

- *Classify* objects, facts or any information.

- *Discriminate* between allied substances or concepts.

- *Identify* relationship between various facts and concepts.

- *Extrapolate* for known information.

- *Translate* symbolic statement into verbal statement and vice versa.

- *Interpret* data, charts, graphs etc.

- *Detect* errors in faculty statements.

- *Verify* facts.

- *Solve* numerical problems.

Application

The essence of teaching learning, as you know, is the application of knowledge. You perform various activities or solve many problems in your daily life. You are able to do this only because you have the knowledge and understanding of the things around yourself. The third objective aims at using knowledge in new situations. It states: "To develop the ability to apply knowledge of concepts and principles of science in new or unfamiliar situations."

Behaviour specification of the objectives is that the pupil will:

- *Analyze* situation or problem

- *Formulate* hypothesis on the basis of observations

- *Select* appropriate methods and material for testing the hypothesis

- *Give reasons* for happenings

- *Draw inferences,* conclusions and generalizations

- *Predict* results or happenings on the basis of known facts

Skills

We know that 'Science learning is science doing', therefore, for learning science, various skills are required for performing activities and acquiring knowledge. Also, type of knowledge acquired by an individual depends upon the processes applied for acquiring it. The fourth objective of teaching science states: "To develop observational, experimental, manipulative and drawing skills".

To demonstrate the acquisition of skills pupil will

- Handle objects, Material, Instruments, Specimens and apparatus properly.

- Clean apparatus and instruments carefully

- Observe and record relevant data accurately

- Measure weight, volume, temperature, pressure and other dimensions accurately

- Put articles in proper order and place

- Draw and label neat and appropriate diagrams

- Make graphs and charts from given data

- Improvise apparatus

- Dissect neatly

- Take precautions

Interest and Appreciation for Science

Why have you studied science? It was because you liked it, you enjoyed studying it, you're curious nature got satisfied by the answers give11 by science. Now you want to develop the same interest and appreciation for science among your students. Pupils learn only when they enjoy the subject and appreciate the fruits of science for the development of society. So, our next objective states: "To develop the power of appreciation of the developments in science and to create interests in learning science."

The behaviour specifications which will be demonstrated by the students on achieving the objectives are that the pupil will be able to:

- Show thrill and excitement while performing science experiments.

- Feel satisfaction in collecting and exhibiting the materials, ob.jects, specimens and the pictures showing development of science.

- Enjoy performing experiments in chemistry.

- Read scientific literature.

- Read with interest, about the achievements and sacrifices of great scientists.

- Take part in scientific debates, discussions and functions.

- Explain interdependence of organism and environment and of organisms themselves.

- Collect materials and specimens.

- Preserves materials. Leaves: flowers, insect's stones and minerals etc., properly.

- Visit places of scientific interest on his own.

- Contribute articles on topics of scientific interest.

- Joins scientific lobby clubs.

- Improvise models and apparatus.

Scientific Attitude

We aspire for the development of scientific attitude ill our students. It is the ultimate aim of science teaching. You will also agree that if we teach science properly i.e, through activities performed under the supervision of teachers or allow children to perform unsupervised activities on their own, then surely they will adopt scientific process for learning their environment. Through guided and self-learning they will acquire the behaviour and attitude which we call as scientific attitude.

Acquiring scientific attitude pupils will demonstrate the following behaviour:

- They will respect the teacher.

- They will have a keen desire to know how's and whys of any event or phenomenon.

- They will not ignore any detail even if it is of no direct relevance of the work in hand.

- They will record, report and interpret their observations honestly.

- They will not accept or reject anything without valid reasons.

- They will suspend judgement till it is repeatedly confirmed.

- They are unbiased in their approach to problems.

- They are willing to consider new ideas and discoveries.

- They will admit their mistakes unhesitatingly.

- They will develop independent thinking.

- They will show a spirit of team work, self-help and self-reliance.

- They are prepared to face hazards in their investigation.

1.6 Values of teaching Chemistry

Intellectual Value of teaching Chemistry

Intellectual virtues are qualities of mind and character that promote intellectual flourishing, critical thinking, and the pursuit of truth. These are important to our young people as they prepare them for further education and future careers.

Creativity: Creativity is the interaction between the learning environment, both physical and social, the attitudes and attributes of both teachers and students, and a clear problem-solving process which produces a perceptible product

Open-mindedness: An open mind — the eagerness to expose oneself to new experiences, beliefs, values, perspectives, etc. That differ from one's own — enables a child to explore how diverse people across the globe think and act

Rational thinking: Rational thinking is the ability to consider, access, organize, and analyze relevant information and then arrive at a systematic conclusion. Through this process, children can sort out different ideas, pick aspects they like best and also voice their opinions more confidently

Empiricism: It is in contexts focusing on influencing learning – in particular, through active, experience-focused, exploration-oriented activities. Concisely, then, within education, Empiricism is frequently engaged as a theory of influencing learning.

Skepticism: Acting as a health skeptic means that students will think critically, and doubt or question everything long after they've left your classroom. To continue to build this thinking, design thinking provides a powerful opportunity to embed this in instruction.

Utilitarian Value of teaching Chemistry

Chemistry is a branch of Natural science that deals principally with the properties of substances, the changes they undergo, and the natural laws that describe these changes. Utilitarian value is that scientific knowledge that is useful in day to day life.

➢ Chemistry plays an important role and useful role towards the development and growth of a number of industries.

➢ This includes industries like glass, cement, paper, textiles, leather, dye etc. We also see huge applications of chemistry in industries like Paints, Pigments, Petroleum, Sugar, Plastics and Pharmaceuticals.

- ➢ The chemical sciences will likely be increasingly required to solve challenges in health, energy and climatic change water and food production.

- ➢ Chemistry might have a greater role in Biochemistry and pharmaceutical industry as well as in the maintenance and development of infrastructure.

- ➢ General chemistry is the study of matter, energy and the interactions between the two. The main topics in chemistry include acids and bases, atomic structure, the periodic table, chemical bonds and chemical reactions.

- ➢ It helps in building career options.

Chemistry is where every: It is the study of building blocks of our world. Everything you touch, wear, eat or drink is the result of chemical process.

Disciplinary Value of teaching Chemistry

Chemistry is the study of matter and energy and the interaction between them. There are many reasons to study chemistry, even if you aren't pursuing a career in science.

Chemistry is everywhere in the world around you! It's in the food you eat, clothes you wear, water you drink, medicines, air, cleaners... you name it. Chemistry sometimes is called the "central science" because it connects other sciences to each other, such as biology, physics, geology, and environmental science. Here are some of the best reasons to study chemistry.

- Chemistry helps you to understand the world around you. Why do leaves change colour in the fall? Why are plants green? How is cheese made? What is in soap and how does it clean? These are all questions that can be answered by applying chemistry.

- Basic knowledge of chemistry helps you to read and understand product labels.

- Chemistry can help you make informed decisions. Will a product work as advertised or is it a scam? If you understand how chemistry works you'll be able to separate reasonable expectations from pure fiction.

- Chemistry is at the heart of cooking. If you understand the chemical reactions involved in making baked goods rise or neutralizing acidity or thickening sauces, chances are you'll be a better cook.

- A command of chemistry can help keep you safe! You'll know which household chemicals are dangerous to keep together or mix and which can be used safely.

- Chemistry teaches useful skills. Because it is a science, learning chemistry means learning how to be objective and how to reason and solve problems.

- Helps to understand current events, including news about petroleum product, pollution, the environment and technological advances.

- Makes life's little mysteries a little less mysterious. Chemistry explains how things work.

- Chemistry opens up career options. There are many careers in chemistry, but even if you're looking for a job in another field, the analytical skills you gained in chemistry are helpful. Chemistry applies to the food industry, retail sales, transportation, art, homemaking really any type of work you can name.

- Chemistry is fun! There is lots of interesting chemistry projects you can do using common everyday materials. Chemistry projects don't just go boom. They can glow in the dark, change colours, produces bubbles and change states.

Vocational Value of teaching Chemistry

The range of available jobs is considerable and covers many different types of chemistry and industries such as nanotechnology, large scale chemical plants, the drinks and pharmaceutical industries or teaching.

Your skills will also be in demand in other areas. A study of chemistry helps you develop logical thought and numerical skills and the ability to write accurate and concise reports. As a result, our chemists are in demand in national and local government, in hospitals and in education at all levels.

Opportunities include, but are not limited to:

➤ Accountant/ Auditor

➤ Analytical Chemists

➤ Chemical Development Engineer

➤ Chemical Engineers

➤ Chemistry Teachers

➤ Development Chemists

➤ Environmental Chemist

➤ Forensic Examiners

➤ Forensic Researcher

➤ Forensic Scientist

➤ Laboratory Technicians

➤ Patent Agent

➤ Police Officers

> Project Engineers

> Purification Scientist

> Research Analysts

> Technical Associates

> Toxicologist

There are also major opportunities for chemists in non-chemical areas. Studying chemistry helps develop your logical thought, problem solving and numeric skills, and the ability to write accurate and concise reports – all important for a range of jobs. Many Strathclyde chemistry graduates have found interesting and rewarding careers in areas such banking, finance, recruitment, marketing and the civil service.

Cultural Value of teaching Chemistry

It's challenging to quantify the impact of something as big as chemistry on the modern world. It's difficult because there isn't a single aspect of modern life that chemistry doesn't touch in some way, whether it's the phone in your pocket, the shoes you're wearing, or the meal you just ate. Chemistry is an enormous scientific field with millions of practical applications. Let's take a closer look at just a few of the ways chemistry has impacted modern society.

> **Fashion and Clothing:** Most of the fabric in your closet is probably made up of synthetic fibers, meaning man-made fibers

synthesized in a lab. The dyes in your clothes, the detergent you use to wash them, and the bleach that you use to remove stains are all inventions of modern chemistry. Even your shoes are mostly vinyl, a type of plastic created by chemists.

➢ **Building and Furniture Construction:** The world of construction is another sector where chemistry has radically improved things. Imagine trying to keep a fence looking nice without stains or building a home without insulation chemistry invented both of those things. Chemistry is also responsible for the laminates on your floors and sinks, the resins on your bookshelf, and the gas and smoke alarms in your workplace.

➢ **Food and Beverages:** Modern agriculture and cuisine would be impossible without the aid of chemistry. Chemists have invented pesticides and fungicides that help farmers produce enough crops to feed the millions of people in our country. Preservatives keep the food on your pantry shelf from going bad before you can use it. Food scientists invent gluten-free and vegan alternatives to popular foods so everyone can take care of themselves as needed.

➢ **Health and Medicine:** As you can already see from this list, chemistry has impacted modern society in innumerable ways, but nowhere is that impact clearer than in the medical world. Without modern chemistry, millions of people would not have access to insulin, vaccines, and antibiotics.

➢ **A World without Chemistry:** We wouldn't live in a world without modern chemistry. This list shows how important chemistry is, we can't live if we didn't have chemistry:

- Fuel for cars and planes

- Shampoo, deodorant and personal care products

- Smartphones and computers

- Modern paper

1.7 Relating objectives with content units of secondary schools

Instructional objectives

- Instructional objectives are specific, measurable, short-term, observable student behaviours.

- An objective is a description of a performance you want learners to be able to exhibit before you consider them competent.

- An objective describes an intended result of instruction, rather than the process of instruction itself. (Note from: http://www.uams.edu/oed/teaching/objectives.htm)

Tips for writing objectives

1. It depends on what they are used for! Objectives for sequencing a unit plan will be more general than for specifying a lesson plan.

2. Don't make writing objectives tedious, trivial, time-consuming, or mechanical. Keep them simple, unambiguous, and clearly focused as a guide to learning.

3. The purpose of objectives is not to restrict spontaneity or constrain the vision of education in the discipline; but to ensure that learning is focused clearly enough that both students and teacher know what is going on.

4. Express them in terms of student performance, behavior, and achievement, not teacher activity.

5. Three components of an instructional objective:

    1. Identify the type of activity in which competence is required.

    2. Specify the criteria or standards by which competence in the activity will be assessed.

    3. List any conditions or circumstances required for students to meet the objective .

Learning level	Associated action verbs
Knowledge	Recalls, Recognises, Instructs, Repeats,

	Shows
Understanding	See the relationship, Cites illustrations/ gives example, Discriminates, Selects, Compares, Classifies, Detect errors, Rectifies errors, Generalises, Verifies, Explains, States
Application	Predicts, Analyses, Formulates hypothesis, Collects, Selects, Judges, Verifies, Solves, Gives, scientific reasons, Interprets, Suggests
Skill	Checks, Rectifies, Cleans, Sets up, Measures, Records, Accurate, observation, Performs, experiment, Uses materials, Repairing the old materials, Sketches the diagram, Draw graphs, Summarises, bservations, Calculates
Appreciation	Expresses, Derives sense of pleasure
Interest	Reads, Takes, Discusses, Sticks, Asks, Forms, Solves, Participates, Organises, Prepares, Collects, Maintains
Attitude	Listens, Accepts, Examines, Appreciates, Encourages

Questions:

1. Define Chemsitry. What is the nature of Chemsitry?

2. Describe the nature and scope of chemistry

3. Explain the scope of chemistry in the present context?

4. Explain the meaning and scope of chemistry. Write briefly the contributions of chemistry to any 3 fields.

5. Explain the scope of chemistry with special reference to its contribution to the field of A) Agriculture B) Medicine C) Industry

6. How chemistry is useful in daily life?

7. What is chemistry? Explain the scope of chemistry with special reference to its contribution to society

8. What are the contributions of chemistry to the society?

9. Explain briefly contributions of any two Indian scientists to the field of chemistry.

10. Explain the contributions of Indian chemists for the development of science.

11. What are the different objectives of teaching chemistry at the secondary stage of education? Suggest the measures to achieve any three of them.

12. List out the important objectives of teaching chemistry at the secondary stage. Explain them briefly. What measures would you suggest to achieve any three of them?

13. What are the objectives of teaching chemistry at secondary school level? Explain with behavioural terms how do you achieve any four of them in brief.

14. Write three application level instructional objectives to the topic 'states of matter'.

15. List out the differences between Ionic bond ad Covalent bond.

16. Utilitarian value of teaching chemsistry

17. Explain any three values of teaching chemistry.

18. What are the values of teaching chemistry? Explain any two of them in the present context.

19. Describe the intellectual and utilitarian values of teaching chemistry.

20. Write three specifications each for "Knowledge" and "Understanding" objectives of teaching chemistry.

21. Write six instructional objectives for a topic of your choice from chemistry.

UNIT II- Planning for teaching chemical science

2.1 Lesson Plan: Meaning, importance and steps

A lesson plan is a teacher's daily guide for what students need to learn, how it will be taught and how learning will be measured.

Lesson plans help teachers be more effective in the classroom by providing a detailed outline to follow each class period.

Lesson plan is teacher's mental and emotional visualization of class room activities.

A lesson plan is a teaching outline of the important points of a lesson arranged in order in which they are to be presented. It may include objectives, points to be asked, references to materials, assignments etc.

A lesson plan is actually a plan of action. It therefore

- Includes the working philosophy of the teacher

- His knowledge of philosophy

- His information about and understanding of his pupils

- His comprehension of the objectives of education

- His knowledge of the material to be taught

- His ability to utilize effective methods

Importance of Lesson Plan

- It helps the teacher to be systematic and orderly in his teaching process.

- It helps to face challenging questions in the class.

- It builds up definite aim for each day's work.

- It gives confidence and self reliance.

- It helps in finishing the lesson in the allotted time.

- It gives good idea to use the teaching aids effectively.

- It helps the teacher to select appropriate method to teach a particular unit.

- It gives chances for good correlation with other subjects and life situation.

- It gives an idea of how questions can be framed involving reflective thinking.

- It helps to get thorough knowledge when they prepare the lesson plan in advance.

Steps of Lesson Plan

A detailed and step-by-step tutorial for drafting a lesson plan can be very beneficial for new teachers or looking for a better way to formulate a lesson plan.

1. **Identify the learning objectives:** Be prepared for the lesson you are to deliver. The goal can be based on what students will

learn by the end of the lesson or how much students memorise and recall when the lesson is over.

2. **Planning activities:** Delivering lectures is a monotonous way of teaching, and students may lose their focus midway. It is, therefore, essential to include learning activities that keep the students engaged and, at the same time, help their learning process.

3. **Collect learning materials:** Some lessons require external supplies like graphs, calculators, or anything else related to the lesson. Pre-planning helps in instructing the students in advance to bring their study materials.

4. **Note down the teaching process:** You may forget a few points while delivering lectures or be unable to follow your teaching methodology. Analyse the students' learning styles in your class to form strategies that can help teach them more efficiently.

5. **Organise your work:** Align all the lesson plan elements using sticky notes, highlighting important and challenging tasks while leaving space for extra inputs while delivering lessons.

6. **Assigning tasks:** It is crucial to hold a small question-answer round, give homework and hold surprise tests simultaneously to analyse the students' learning. It will help the teachers determine if any changes to their teaching style are needed. Keep a note of the assigned tasks to make notes on the average overall class performance.

7. **Assessment of tasks:** The assessment process helps identify the lesson plan's effectiveness. The time taken to complete homework, the overall score, and responsiveness in class are a few metrics that support teachers. Note it down at the end of every lesson.

2.2 Planning and use of ICT and 5E lesson plan

ICT based lesson plan

Infusing ICT (Information and Communication Technology) into lesson planning is a detailed and systematic process that involves integrating digital tools, resources, and strategies into your teaching to enhance the learning experience.

Steps of ICT based lesson plan

8. **Identify Learning Objectives**: Start with clear and specific learning objectives. What do you want your students to learn or achieve by the end of the lesson?

9. **Select Appropriate ICT Tools**: Identify ICT tools and resources that align with your learning objectives. These can include:

   - **Software and Applications**: Choose educational software, apps, or online tools that support your lesson goals.

   - **Multimedia**: Utilize images, videos, animations, and interactive multimedia to engage students.

- **Websites and Online Resources**: Incorporate relevant websites, e-books, articles, and databases for research and exploration.

- **Learning Management Systems (LMS)**: Use an LMS to manage content, assignments, and assessments.

- **Collaboration and Communication Tools**: Employ platforms for discussions, group projects, and communication.

10. **Content Development**: Create or curate digital content that aligns with your lesson objectives. This may include presentations, e-learning modules, or multimedia resources.

11. **Interactive Presentations**: Use presentation software (e.g., PowerPoint, Google Slides, Prezi) to design engaging and visually appealing lesson materials. Incorporate multimedia elements to make the content interactive.

12. **Digital Resources**: Provide links to online resources that supplement the lesson. Ensure that these resources are credible, relevant, and accessible to students.

13. **Collaborative Learning**: Foster collaboration among students using online discussion boards, group projects, and collaborative tools such as Google Docs or Microsoft Teams.

14. **Assessment Tools**: Incorporate digital assessment tools like online quizzes, surveys, and self-assessment activities for formative and summative assessments.

15. **Adaptive Learning**: Consider adaptive learning platforms that personalize content and assignments based on individual student needs and progress.

16. **Feedback Mechanisms**: Use ICT tools for efficient and timely feedback. Learning management systems often offer features for automated grading and feedback.

17. **Monitoring and Analytics**: Utilize data analytics and LMS dashboards to monitor student progress. Analyze the data to identify areas where students may need additional support or content adjustments.

18. **Multimedia Integration**: Integrate various multimedia elements like audio and video to cater to different learning styles and engage students visually and auditorily.

19. **Virtual Labs and Simulations**: In science and technical subjects, consider virtual labs and simulations that allow students to conduct experiments and practice skills in a virtual environment.

20. **Flipped Classroom Approach**: Consider using ICT to deliver content outside of class, allowing in-class time for discussions, problem-solving, and collaborative activities.

21. **Accessibility and Inclusivity**: Ensure that all ICT tools and content are accessible to all students, including those with disabilities. Use technologies that offer features like closed captions, screen readers, and alternative formats.

22. **Professional Development**: Teachers may need training and ongoing professional development to effectively use ICT in lesson planning. Many educational institutions offer workshops and resources for this purpose.

23. **Continuous Improvement**: Continuously evaluate the effectiveness of ICT integration in lesson planning. Collect feedback from students and use data analytics to make improvements.

Importance of ICT based lesson plan

- Easy to prepare

- Easy to edit or modify

- Repetition can be avoided

- Printing and distribution become easier

- Comparision is possible

- Useful for record keeping

- Unambiguousness of meaning

- Enhanced impact

- Time efforts can be saved

CCE / 5E based lesson plan

Continuous and Comprehensive Evaluation (CCE) was a process of assessment, mandated by the Right to Education Act, of India in 2009.

Continuous and Comprehensive Evaluation (CCE) was a process of assessment, mandated by the Right to Education Act, of India in 2009.

This approach to assessment was introduced by state governments in India, as well as by the Central Board of Secondary Education in India, for students of sixth to tenth grades and twelfth in some schools.

The main aim of CCE was to evaluate every aspect of the child during their presence at the school.

As a part of this system, students' marks were replaced by grades which were evaluated through a series of curricular and extra-curricular evaluations along with academics.

Steps of CCE based Lesson Plan

When planning a lesson each of these areas should be completed. The **5 E**s are:

- ➤ Engage
- ➤ Explore
- ➤ Explain
- ➤ Elaborate
- ➤ Evaluate

Engage

> To engage means to excite and to draw student's curiosity.

> It is not forcing children to learn, but inviting them to do so. This is how lessons are to be introduced.

> Using technology to engage students, like using Smartboard technology, videos, illustrations, asking questions, charts, reading a book, acting out a character or even introducing a game are ways to engage students at the beginning of a lesson. To prepare students mind to receive new knowledge.

In simpler words, Capture student attention, activate student prior knowledge, stimulate thinking, raise key questions, etc.

Engage	Teacher behavior	Student behavior
> Generate interest > Access prior knowledge > Connect to past knowledge > Set parameters of the focus > Frame the idea	> Motivates > Creates interest > Taps into what students know or think about the topic > Raises questions and encourages responses	> Attentive in listening > Ask questions > Demonstrates interest in the lesson > Responds to questions demonstrating their own entry point of understanding

Explore

During the Explore stage students should be given opportunities to work together without direct instruction from the teacher.

During the Explore stage students should be given opportunities to work together without direct instruction from the teacher.

You should act as a facilitator helping students to frame questions by asking questions and observing.

This is the opportunity for students to test predictions and hypotheses and/or form new ones, try alternatives and discuss them with peers, record observations and ideas and suspend judgment.

In simpler words, allow students to observe, record data, isolate variables, design and plan experiments, create graphs, interpret results, develop hypotheses, and organize their findings.

Explore	Teacher behavior	Student behavior
➢ Experience key concepts ➢ Discover new skills ➢ Probe, inquire and question experiences ➢ Examine their thinking	➢ Acts as a facilitator Observes and listens to students as they interact ➢ Asks good inquiry oriented questions	➢ Conducts activities, predicts, and forms hypotheses or makes generalizations ➢ Becomes a good listener

➢ Establish relationships and understanding	➢ Provides time for students to think and to reflect ➢ Encourages cooperative learning	➢ Shares ideas and suspends judgment ➢ Records observations and/or generalizations ➢ Discusses tentative alternatives

Explain

During the Explain stage, Teacher should encourage students to explain, narrate, describe the concepts in their own words, ask for evidence and clarification of their explanation, listen critically to one another's explanation.

Students should use observations and recordings in their explanations.

At this stage you should provide definitions and explanations using students' previous experiences as a basis for the discussion.

In simpler words, Introduce laws, models, theories, and vocabulary. Guide students toward coherent generalizations and help students understand and use scientific vocabulary to explain the results of their explorations.

Explain	Teacher behavior	Student behavior
<ul><li>Connect prior knowledge and background to new discoveries</li><li>Communicate new understandings</li><li>Connect informal language to formal language</li></ul>	<ul><li>Encourages students to explain their observations and findings in their own words</li><li>Provides definitions, new words, and explanations</li><li>Listens and builds upon discussion form students</li><li>Asks for clarification and justification</li><li>Accepts all reasonable responses</li></ul>	<ul><li>Explains, listens, defines, and questions</li><li>Uses previous observations and findings</li><li>Provides reasonable responses to questions</li><li>Interacts in a positive, supportive manner</li></ul>

Elaborate / Extend

> During the Extend stage, students should apply concepts and skills in new (but similar) situations and use formal labels and definitions.

> Remind students of alternative explanations and to consider existing data and evidence as they explore new situations.

> Explore strategies apply here as well because students should be using the previous information to ask questions, propose solutions, make decisions, experiment, and record observations.

In simpler words, Provide students opportunity to apply their knowledge to new domains, raise new questions, and explore new hypotheses. May also include related problems for students to solve.

Elaborate	Teacher behavior	Student behavior
➢ Apply new learning to a new or similar situation ➢ Extend and explain concept being explored ➢ Communicate new understanding with formal language ➢ Application and Problem solving	➢ Uses previously learned information as a vehicle to enhance additional learning ➢ Encourages students to apply or extend the new concepts and skills ➢ Encourages students to use terms and definitions previously acquired	➢ Applies new terms and definitions ➢ Uses previous information to probe, ask questions and make reasonable judgments ➢ Provides reasonable conclusions and solutions ➢ Records observations, explanations and solutions

Evaluate

➢ Evaluation should take place throughout the learning experience.

➢ You should observe students' knowledge and/or skills, application of new concepts and a change in thinking.

➢ Students should assess their own learning. Ask open-ended questions and look for answers that use observation, evidence, and previously accepted explanations.

➢ Ask questions that would encourage future investigations.

Evaluate	Teacher behavior	Student behavior
➢ Assess understanding (Self, peer and teacher evaluation) ➢ Demonstrate understanding of new concept by observation or open ended response ➢ Apply within problem situation ➢ Show evidence of accomplishment	➢ Observes student behaviors as they explore and apply new concepts and skills ➢ Assesses students' knowledge and skills ➢ Encourages students to assess their own learning ➢ Asks open-ended questions	➢ Demonstrates an understanding or knowledge of concepts and skills ➢ Evaluates his/her own progress ➢ Answers open-ended questions ➢ Provides reasonable responses and explanations to events or phenomena

Importance of 5E lesson plan

1. Promotes Active Learning

Engage: The initial phase captures students' interest and stimulates their curiosity. By posing questions or presenting a problem, it encourages students to actively think and inquire about the topic.

Explore: Students engage in hands-on activities or experiments, allowing them to investigate concepts in a practical and interactive manner.

2. Encourages Inquiry-Based Learning

Exploration: Students investigate and experiment with concepts, which foster inquiry-based learning. This approach encourages students to develop their own understanding and solutions.

Questioning: The model supports the development of critical thinking by encouraging students to ask questions and seek answers through investigation.

3. Facilitates Deep Understanding

Explain: After exploring, students articulate their understanding and receive explanations from the teacher. This phase helps consolidate their knowledge and correct misconceptions.

Conceptual Clarity: The explanation phase allows for deeper comprehension and clarification of concepts, promoting better retention and understanding.

4. Supports Differentiated Instruction

Flexible Activities: The 5E model provides multiple entry points for students with different learning styles and abilities. The engage and explore phases offer various ways for students to connect with the material.

Adaptable: Teachers can adjust the activities and explanations based on individual student needs, ensuring that all students can access and understand the content.

5. Encourages Application of Knowledge

Elaborate: Students apply what they've learned to new situations, which reinforce their understanding and helps them make connections to real-world contexts.

Transfer of Learning: By applying concepts in different scenarios, students develop the ability to transfer their knowledge to new problems or situations.

6. Promotes Continuous Assessment

Evaluate: The final phase involves assessing students' understanding and providing feedback. This ongoing evaluation helps teachers gauge student progress and adjust instruction as needed.

Reflective Practice: Evaluation encourages both students and teachers to reflect on learning outcomes and instructional effectiveness.

7. Fosters Collaborative Learning

Group Activities: The explore and elaborate phases often involve collaborative activities that promote teamwork, communication, and problem-solving skills.

Peer Learning: Students can learn from each other's perspectives and insights, enhancing their overall understanding of the topic.

8. Enhances Student Motivation

Interactive Engagement: The engaging activities in the initial phases capture students' interest and motivation, making learning more enjoyable and relevant.

Real-World Connections: By linking learning to real-world problems and applications, students see the relevance of their studies, increasing their motivation to learn.

9. Provides Structured Learning

Clear Phases: The 5E model provides a clear, structured framework for lesson planning and delivery, ensuring that all critical aspects of learning are addressed.

Sequential Learning: The model's sequential phases guide students through a logical progression of learning, from initial engagement to final evaluation.

2.3 Unit Plan: Meaning, importance, components and steps

Planning is necessary in every field. To plan means to **"To act with a Purpose".** No teacher should enter the class without planning. Planning of a lesson is related to the working philosophy of the teacher. Educational objectives, methods and techniques used and relating educational objectives.

Unit planning or Approach is associated with professor **H.C.Morrison** of the University of Chicago. It is described of teaching in secondary schools published in 1926. Unit Plan is very popular and frequently used in USA. It is based on field theories of learning or Holistic outlook. The Idea behind it is that the learner has to react to the situation as a whole and not the parts in isolation. A Unit is a part of the whole.

According to Prerton: "A Unit is a large block on related subject matter as can be overviewed by the learner".

According to Bossing: "A unit consists of a comprehensive series of related and meaningful activities so as to achieve pupils' purpose, provides significant learning experiences and result in appropriate behavioral changes.

According to Hoover: Unit plan is group of related concepts from which a given set of instructional and educational experiences are derived.

According to samford: An outline of carefully related subject matter which has been isolated because of its relationship to pupil needs and interest.

Characteristics of good unit plan

- Aims should be clear and well defined.

- The Teaching aids to be used are clear in unit

- After teaching of that unit there should be provision of evaluation

- It should always be a complete integrated whole in its organization.

- It provides activities for the students.

- It provides correlation with the life,

- They have chance to plan organize and execute there is begin and end in the Unit.

- To keep in mind the need interest capabilities of students level and Knowledge of students.

- It should be based on previous experiences of the students.

- The length of the Unit should sustain the Interest of the students up to the last. It should not be too long nor too short.

- The Unit should not be below two periods and above seven periods.

- The unit should contain familiar and selected aspects unit should not be remote. It should be related to previous knowledge.

Steps for developing unit plan

> Preparation/ Motivation

> Knowing Previous knowledge

> Presentation

> Organization

- ➢ Summarization

- ➢ Drill or Recapitulation

- ➢ Evaluation

Preparation/ Motivation: It is just to motivate the students for learning. This spirit should be maintained not only in the beginning but also till the end of the lesson.

Knowing the Previous knowledge: "Start with the pupils where they are" is the modern slogan in education. It is essential to know about the background of the students. So that neither there is duplication of what they already have nor any danger of having anything in the unit is above the comprehensive of the students.

Presentation: Subject matter is present to the students with the help of aids or direct or indirect experiences. In order to add new experiences to the knowledge the students.

Organization of Learning: The Students get an opportunities to bring their learning together so that they may establish relationship between the new experiences and assimilated one.

Summarization: This is usually required at the close of the teaching unit to bring all the learning. This may also be done at intervals during the progress of unit organization and summarizations go together.

Drill: For this review just revision of the new experiences taught, during the presentation is required some learning experiences acquire repetition. It is called as drill. Review and drill may also be required at a number of places during the lesson.

Evaluation: This required knowing what the students have achieved and what they have failed to achieve. Evaluation should be mainly self-evaluation. This may be in the form of oral or written tests after short intervals.

Advantages of Unit Plan

- It provides basic course structure around which specific class activates can be organized.

- It is based on Gestalt psychology of learning theory

- Since the subject matter is divided into sub units, it helps for easy comprehension.

- It develops understanding and an objective approach

- All the steps are directed to achieve the desire of the goals and Mastery.

- It facilitates proper interaction between the learner and teacher.

- Learning process is organizing systematic and logical.

- It employs democracy in the class room.

- It enables the teacher to break away from traditional text book teaching.

Demerits of Unit Plan

- It is supposed to be time consuming.

- It is more suited to intelligent students.

- It puts heavy demand on the teachers.

- Some teachers adopt it without understanding what it is and how it is to be used.

- School time table is already over crowed, it is not possible to organize and finish the syllabus.

- This method requires supplementary reading materials; school tacks sufficient text books periodicals.

2.4 Resource Unit: Meaning, Components, Steps and Importance.

A Resource Unit is a reservoir containing collection of materials, resources, problems, projects, activities, biographies, etc. related to an area of topic which of topic which a teacher uses in planning, developing and evaluating a learning unit.

It's a teacher guide to planning and action or it is a handbook for teachers, generally it contains more information about the topic than needed.

Definitions of Resource Unit

Resource Unit is defined as Comprehensive collection of suggested learning activities procedure, material and references organised around unifying topic or learner's problem.

- Dictionary of Education

A Resources Unit is a comprehensive collection of suggested teaching and learning activities around unified topic or learning problem designed to be helpful to teachers in developing their own teaching units appropriate to their respective classes.

-Regional College of Education

Collection of materials, activities and resources related to an area of topic organised traditional way which a teacher uses in planning and developing of the Unit.

-Edrist

Resource Unit is one of the instructional materials which play a vital role in enhancing the quantity of Education.

Importance of Resource Unit

1. Resource Unit is a Teacher guide for planning and action. It's a collection of information regarding a particular Unit.

2. Provides experience to students that leads to reflective thinking.

3. It explores the importance of community resources to students.

4. Improves the knowledge of the students.

5. Gives information to both the students and teachers.

6. Co-relates the subjects with the others.

7. Acts as guide to the students about the particular topic.

8. Useful for successful teaching

9. Provides extra information to both the teacher and students other than the matter present in the topic.

Characteristics of Resources Unit

1. It stimulates the learning in students.

2. Resource Unit is prepared by the team of trained teachers.

3. It influences the teachers in preparing a lesson plan and in giving guidance as well as improving the plan at every stage.

4. Helps in planning effective evaluation techniques, teaching aids, to find remedies to problem in learning process.

5. It is helpful in preparing the plan according to student maturity.

6. It provides suitable socialising activities.

7. It contains the various suggested activities related to topic

Advantages of Resource Unit

1. Teachers can make use of it while developing their own teaching Unit. The matter and materials have been brought together organised in the general pattern.

2. Teachers may draw upon it for extensive suggestions and regard it as a kind of reference materials and developing his own teaching Unit for his class.

3. It may be employed to provide a unified approach to some particular problem

4. It works as a practical stock house for teachers.

5. It makes teaching learning process effective.

6. It determines the work system, means which unit and which subunit is taught and which aid is to be used.

Disadvantages of Resource Unit

1. The resource Unit includes many concepts, sometimes this may leads to confusion for students.

2. Since the topics are many, it cannot be taught in a particular time.

3. It is time consuming for single topic.

4. Preparation of Resource Unit requires Communication, dedication and service mindedness of Teachers.

5. Preparation of Resource Unit is laborious.

2.5 Chemistry laboratory: importance, designing, planning, equipping, maintenance of equipment and records.

The laboratory is commonly regarded as the heart of science teaching. The science laboratory provides opportunities to the pupils to understand the concepts and different ideas of science.

"Science laboratory is the central place where students get an opportunity to conduct experiments and search principles of science".

The laboratory helps in the development of objective reasoning and thinking, skills of experimentation, observation, problem solving and scientific attitudes among the students.

Location and Types of Science Laboratories

A science laboratory should be located preferably on the school building if possible so that there is no disturbance of the laboratory. The open space outside the laboratory will be of much use to conduct some of the experiments outside, in sunlight. Biology and general science laboratory should have north-south orientation to provide adequate sunlight exposure.

There are three important plans of science laboratory

1. Lecture room - cum - laboratory plan.

2. Lecture - cum - laboratory plan.

These two plans are a combined one with a lecture room and a laboratory attached side by side. Half of the whole laboratory is used as lecture room and half as a laboratory to arrange practical classes for one or more subjects.

3. All-purpose laboratory:

The whole laboratory is used for all purposes namely for lecture and laboratory work.

Planning a Science Laboratory

Before constructing the science laboratory, the following factors should be taken into consideration at the planning stage.

➢ The number of pupils working at a time.

➢ The minimum space necessary for each pupil for comfortable working.

➢ Limitations of number of science teachers in secondary schools.

➢ Need for ancillary accommodation for storage.

➢ Designing the science class-room and laboratory in such a way that it could be used for science teaching for middle as well as for high classes.

➢ Imperative need for economy.

Chemistry Laboratory

Location: It should be preferably on the ground floor.

Lay out: It should be 45 feet x 25 feet for a class of 40 students in demonstration and 20 for practical classes. One door should be near demonstration table of the teacher and the other at the other end. Windows preferably with wire gauze should be provided, and should open outside. They should be 6' x 8'.

Ventilation: In chemistry experiments heat is required in carrying out almost all experiments. Moreover gases give nauseating smell. So ventilation should be there. Ventilators should be provided with exhaust fans. Without them conditions might become intolerable for students to work.

Walls: The walls may be about 1½ feet thick. Painting should be done or annual white washing is should be done.

Floors: They should be cemented. Slight slope helps in sweeping. Round corners prevent the dust from being accumulated.

Water Supply: Water supply is different in different places, depending upon the source of water supply. It is preferable if storage tank is built on the roof of science laboratory.

Gas Supply: Gas supply may be provided by means of petrol gas plants which are easy to operate and maintain. The gas plant must be installed outside the laboratory. Each burner should have individual gas control knob.

Work Tables: Single work table of dimensions 1.5m x 0.75m x 0.75m is ideal for individual practical classes. The tables must be arranged so that the teacher can easily see from his demonstration table what every student is doing.

Sink: Sinks must be provided in each work table in the chemistry laboratory where the students would have to clean the test tubes very often.

Demonstration Table: A long table preferably raised by means of a small platform should be provided in each laboratory at one end. The demonstration table must be provided with water supply and gas supply.

Blackboard and Bulletin board: A black board must be fitted on the wall just behind the demonstration table, so that the teacher can use it during demonstration. There must be a notice board inside the laboratory near the entrance door.

Cupboards, Fire Extinguishers and First Aid Box: There must be enough number of cupboards or almirahs to store things and chemicals. There must be at least two fire extinguishers and one first aid box in the laboratory.

Storeroom: In addition to the materials kept in the laboratory, materials which are costly and needing special care can be stored in the store room.

Purchase of apparatus and equipments

Sufficient materials, apparatus and equipment are essential for any laboratory. A list of all the required apparatus, tools, equipment, chemicals, reagents etc., should be prepared and purchased from the scientific stores.

Procedure for the Purchase

Preparation of the indent: Based on the grant and the immediate requirement either for getting a new laboratory or for a laboratory already established the list of articles equipment are to be prepared and they should be assorted into different categories. The indent should be prepared in duplicate and it should be sent to the concerned higher authorities for approval. The approved indent, with required particulars should be sent to more than three approved scientific companies asking for the price of the articles in the indent which they can supply.

Preparation of comparative statement: After receiving the quotations from at least three companies the comparative statement can be prepared. While considering the quotations the quality also should be compared and considered. Quality should not suffer at the cost of money. The company that has offered the lowest quotation is given the order to supply the materials when asking for quotations we have to give specifications.

For example if we simply say dissection box one may give the rate for that made up of iron while the other may give it for stainless steel. Naturally the rate for the iron will be less and we should be going for the purchase of it and suffer later.

Placement of orders: The teacher through the headmaster should place the order of the articles to the respective companies which have offered the lowest rate. While placing the orders the time specification also should be clearly mentioned, so that they are received in time and utilized by the students.

Receipt of the articles: When the articles are received the price list is to be compared with that of the quotation to find out whether the price is the same. If there is any discrepancy, deficiency or damage if should be immediately communicated to the respective company and arrangement should be made to return the item and get a new one or reduce the price in the bill. It is advisable to get the costly article and glass wares insured against any damage. Then only the bill should be recommended for payment.

Stock registers

The apparatus purchased should be properly checked and entered. A stock register is used for the entry of items received and also to maintain a record of science apparatus. It helps in knowing the position of apparatus, chemicals and also helps while auditing. The science teacher should maintain the following registers in the laboratory.

(i) Accessing register

After receiving and checking the working conditions all the articles irrespective of consumable or non-consumable are entered in this register. The register should have the following format.

Date of purc hase	Bill No. & name of company	Descrip tion of articles	Qty.	Cost	Page No. in the relevant stock register	Rem arks

(ii)   Non-consumable register

Articles of permanent nature which are not liable to be broken are to be entered in this register. The article such as sonometer, magnets, spectrometer, electrical appliances and instruments, balances etc should be entered in this register. The register should have the following format.

Date of purc hase	Bill No. & name of compan y	Descri ption of articles	Qty. recei ved	No. brok en, remo ved	Ba lan ce	Remar ks & initial

It is preferable to enter the articles in the alphabetical order. It is better to enter each type of article in separate pages. Articles if broken accidentally or during use should be removed from this register with the permission of the competent authority. Such removal must always have the sanction of the competent authority in writing.

(iii) Consumable register

Articles which are likely to be broken very often and articles which have to be thrown out after use can be entered in this stock registers. For example test tubes, glass rods, glass tubes, rubber tubes, litmus paper, corks, chemicals, dry cells, bulbs, extension wire, oil, fuse wire etc. have to be entered in this. The teacher has the power to write off such articles from this register. Any such removal need not have any sanction from the higher authority. The format of the register will be as follows.

Date of purchase	Bill No. and name of company	Description of articles	Qty. Received	Issued or removed	Balance	Remarks and initial

It is better to allot one page to one type of article so that additions and deletions in future can be noted on the same page.

(iv) Issue register

Whenever an article is issued to other department or teacher, it should be entered in the issue register with date and number. After it is returned it should be entered after verifying the working condition of the article.

(v)   Breakage register

Articles which are broken by the students and others while doing the practical work and demonstration should be entered in this register and later one can be removed from the concerned stock register.

Organization of practical work

It is essential for a science teacher to complement her class room lessons to the practical work conducted in the lab. The success of the practical work depends on the planning and the organisation. In the organisation of the practical work, time scheduling and the actual practical work are the components.

Time Scheduling

The mental process involved in practical is not different from theoretical work. The time required for each experiment may differ depending on the nature of the practical.

- Time is needed to prepare the material before the practical commences.

- Practical procedures occupy different lengths of time.

- Pupils need time for the preparation of the practical work, to sharpen the scalpels or get the apparatus.

- Time should be allotted for the demonstration.

- Time should be scheduled according to the working rates of the students.

> The facts of the psychological mechanism 'repetitive experiences is often more effective than single experience' should be considered.

Organising the Work of the Practical Class

All the preparatory works should be completed before the practical begins and the students should know before hand what work they are to do and should be prepared with the appropriate instruments, instructional materials such as work sheets and apparatus should be ready. After the arrangements the teacher should demonstrate what is to be done. During the demonstration the purpose should be defined, its method explained and its results shown but during the process itself there should be the cut and thrust of question and answer. When the process is to continue after giving the brief description of the whole process, conveniently it can be done in stages.

Guidelines for Teachers in Organizing Practical Work

> The teacher should conduct demonstrations and also provide the students with instruction cards containing information about the experiments to be performed. It provides clarity to the students and saves time.

> The experiments should be properly done. Accurate readings should be noted down.

> In the record books, the data and the diagrams should be entered. The calculations should be worked out.

- Teacher should check and sign every students practical book after the completion of the experimental work at the end of the practical session.

- Teachers should explain the care and accuracy of apparatus to the students.

- Teacher may be flexible and innovative in devising new methods or procedures, while working with large groups or with limited supply of chemicals and apparatus.

- Teacher should be cautious about accidents in the lab and in case of accident he should provide first aid to the victims immediately.

Laboratory Records of Students

- The records serve as self learning materials for the students. In the records they are able to condense and organize the matter. The records are the means to convey what they know about the concepts of the experiments. The students should be properly trained to record the experiments that they perform in the laboratory.

- The teacher should make the students to enter each and every observation directly into their fair note books. Recording on the rough notebook and copying later should be avoided.

- The procedures for the experiment should be on the right side while the observed information should be recorded on the left side appropriately. The use of printed records should be avoided as they may contain unnecessary and more information. The method of doing the experiment and the recording pattern may be different.

> Always the procedure should be written in passive voice and not in active voice or in the order form.

Laboratory Manual

A laboratory manual is an essential guide to laboratory work. It is a book that gives guidelines for doing practical. It gives good practical guidance regarding the procedure, observation and precaution. It is always better to follow the lab manual for systematic conduct of experimental work.

The laboratory manual provides:

> The aim of the experiment

> The apparatus and chemicals required.

> The method or the procedure followed

> The formula for analysis

> Precautions for effective wor

> Illustration for the experiment

In the manual the different experiments are described with appropriate figures and tabulations and help the student to complete the record works. Wherever necessary the diagrams of the apparatus and the format of the tabulations and the procedure of the calculations for the different experiments are given.

Instruction Cards

Instruction cards are small postcard sized cards on which the instructions and guidelines for individual experiments are written. The size of the card is 15cm x 10cm. The instruction card is prepared for each practical and is given to the student before he starts his practical works.

The instruction cards contain

- Procedure
- Method to record the observations / data
- Formulae and the method for calculations.
- Precautions to be taken for proper working.
- The instruction card is preferably covered with a polythene cover.

Benefits of instruction card

- Helps to save the time of the teacher and the student.
- Enables the student to go through it when he gets the doubt.
- Helps to enable the systematic procedure for each experiment.
- Helps the learner to become familiar with the concerned experiment.

> Helps to gather the materials before starting the actual practical.

Safety precautions

A laboratory is a dangerous place if not managed properly as it contains explosive chemicals and reagents, glass wares, poisons etc and with the increasing scientific progress, the corresponding hazards are also increasing. Therefore laboratory safety is the most important task that a science teacher should know. Good laboratory practices are prerequisite for the management of safety in any laboratory. For this purpose certain safety rules should be adopted and strictly followed.

General Safety Rules for the Lab

> The science students should follow the following rules to avoid many accidents in laboratories.

> In case of any accident immediately report to the teacher.

> Work should be done only under the supervision of the teacher.

> Equipment should be handled only after reading the instructions.

> Chemicals should be used only after receiving the instructions and precautions from the teachers.

> Laboratory apparatus should not be used without the permission of the teacher.

- Caution should be taken while handling and pouring chemicals and reagents.

- Never pour back the reagents or chemicals into the bottles.

- Chemicals spilled on the skin should be immediately washed with water.

- Working area should be cleaned before and after the experiment.

- In case of accidents or injuries, first aid should be immediately provided. Therefore, first aid is an important requirement in any science laboratory. The science teacher should be trained in providing first aid to the injured students.

Safety Equipment

- Along with the first aid box every laboratory should be equipped with the following safety equipment also

- fire extinguishers

- rubber gloves

- asbestos safety screens

- Dust bins

- Thick blankets

- Sand blankets, etc.

Some Common Laboratory Mishaps and their Remedies

Cuts: If it is a minor cut, the affected portion should be washed with a weak antiseptic lotion such as diluted 1:10 dettol. Then tincture of iodine on a pad of cotton wool may be applied.

If there is arterial bleeding, a doctor's attention is immediately needed. A thick pad of gauze or cotton wool should be pressed over the wound. Tourniquet may be used to stop the bleeding.

Burns: It is caused by dry heat such as hot iron, hot glass rod, by some acid or alkali, phosphorus or sodium or potassium. For small burns apply sterilized pad of cotton wool or gauge soaked in sodium bicarbonate solution which should be replaced before it gets dried gentian violet jelly may be used. In some cases special procedure is necessary as follows.

Acid burns: Concentrated acids will cause serious burns. The portion affected by acid must be immediately washed with large quantity of water and then treated with a weak solution of sodium bicarbonate to neutralize the acid. Alkali should not be poured over the affected area without washing it with large quantity of water as it will produce excessive heat due to neutralization.

Alkali burns: The affected area must be washed with water and then with 1% solution of acetic acid or lemon juice. Phosphorus burns must be immersed in water and all traces of the substance washed away. The part should then be treated with dilute silver nitrate solution.

Eye injuries: Any injury in the eye must be carefully attended. A drop of oil must be put into the eye.

> **Acid in the eye:** The eye must be washed by a slow stream of water from a wash bottle. It should then be rinsed several times with lime water or 1% solution of sodium bicarbonate.

> **Alkali in the eye:** The eye should be thoroughly washed with water and then with 1% solution of boric acid.

> **Solid in the eye:** Any obvious solid may be removed gently by a camel-hair brush dipped in glycerine.

Poisoning: In all cases of suspected poisoning, the doctor should be consulted soon after the first- aid treatment.

> **Substance taken into the month:** If a poisonous substance either solid or liquid has been taken into the mouth, it should be spit out at once and the mouth rinsed with much water followed by a wash with saturated sodium bicarbonate solution if acid or with 1% acetic acid solution if alkali,

> **Substance swallowed:** In this case the poisoning can be classified into two types.

> – Poisoning due to corrosive substances.

> – Poisoning due to non-corrosive substances.

If the substance swallowed is non-corrosive the patient may be encouraged to vomit. A table spoon full of common salt or a tea spoon full of mustard in warm water will encourage vomiting. Then white egg, rice-water etc. should be given.

If the substance swallowed is corrosive, the patient should not be encouraged to vomit. In the case of acids much water, followed by lime water or milk of magnesia should be drunk. If alkalies, much water followed by dilute acetic and or lime juice should be taken.

In the case of poisonous gases the patient should be taken into fresh air at once, clothing must be loosened and a hot stimulant like coffee should be given.

Fainting: It a pupil feels or looks faint after an accident, his clothing must be loosened and fresh air must be allowed to blow on his face. A little cold water or hot stimulant can be given, when he becomes conscious.

Electric shock: The first thing is to switch off the current. If necessary the pupil should be treated for burns and shock. He should be kept quiet and warm and made to lie down flat. In serious cases artificial respiration may be given.

Fire accidents: In the case of fire the following steps should be followed.

➢ If a pupil's clothes catch fire, he should be wrapped with a blanket immediately.

- ➢ Small fires due to oil, sodium etc can often be put out by putting a large amount of dry sand.

- ➢ If some inflammable substances catch fire, it can be extinguished and prevented from spreading by pressing a sheet of asbestos.

- ➢ If the fire is due to gas or electricity the main source of supply should be cut off first.

- ➢ In all cases of emergency fire buckets filled with sand and water and suitable number of fire extinguishers must be kept ready.

Questions:

1. What is lesson planning? Explain the different steps in planning a lesson.
2. What is lesson plan? Explain the importance of lesson plan.
3. How do you introduce the topic 'Cement'?
4. What is lesson plan? Explain briefly the 5E steps in planning lesson.
5. Write expected learning outcome, teacher-pupil activites and evaluation question for the concept 'periodic table'
6. Write three application level instructional objectives to the topic 'state of matter'.
7. Listout the advantages of writing lesson plans while teaching chemistry.
8. How is unit plan helpful in preparing lesson plans?

9. What is the difference between Lesson plan and Unit plan?

10. How do you introduce the topic 'Chemical Bonding'?

11. Frame four instructional objectives of understanding level to the topic 'Atomic Structure'

12. Suggest suitable learning experiences to be given to teach 'Valency'

13. Give introduction to teach the topic periodic table

14. What is the importance of content analysis in teaching chemistry?

15. What is Unit plan? Briefly explain the steps of Unit plan with a suitable example from chemistry.

16. What is Resource Unit? What are the advantages & disadvantages of resource unit?

17. What is resource Unit? Explain the steps while preparing the resource unit in chemistry. Mention its advantages and limitations.

18. Explain the steps involved in the construction of Resource Unit.

19. What is the importance of chemistry laboratory at the secondary stage? What points would you keep in your mind while designing the laboratory for your school?

20. What are the criteria for setting a good chemistry laboratory? Explain.

21. How to maintenance of apparatus, Chemicals and records in the laboratory?

22. List out the Laboratory records

23. What are the precautions to be taken while using concentrated acids?

UNIT III- Approaches, methods and techniques of teaching chemical science

3.1 Approaches: Teacher centered, Learner centered, Activity centered

"A thousand teachers, a thousand methods" - Chinese Proverb

Teaching approach: It is a set of principles, beliefs, or ideas about the nature of learning which is translated into the classroom.

Teaching strategy: It is a long term plan of action designed to achieve a particular goal.

Teaching method: It is a systematic way of doing something. It implies an orderly logical arrangement of steps. It is more procedural.

Teaching technique: It is a well-defined procedure used to accomplish a specific activity or task.

Teacher Centered Learning

In teacher centred learning the more traditional or conventional approach to teaching. The teacher functions in the familiar role of classroom lecturer, presenting information to the students, who are expected to passively receive the knowledge being presented.

A teacher centred learning environment is one in which:

- The focus is primarily on the instructor

- The teacher chooses the topics

- The teacher talks and the students listen

- What the teacher knows about the subject takes priority

- Students work alone/independently

- The teacher monitors and corrects student work as needed

- The teacher is solely responsible for answering students' questions

- The teacher evaluates students' performance and evidence of learning

- The classroom is typically quiet

Advantages of Teacher Centered Classroom

- Order in the class! The teacher exercises full control of the classroom and activities.

- Being fully in control minimizes an instructor's concern that students may be missing key material.

- When a teacher takes full responsibility for educating a group of students, the class benefits from a focused approach to research, planning and preparation.

- Teachers feel comfortable, confident and in charge of the classroom activities.

- Students always know where to focus their attention on the teacher.

Disadvantages of Teacher Centered Classroom

- This method works best when the instructor can make the lesson interesting; absent this, students may get bored, their minds may wander and they may miss key information.

- Students work alone, missing potential opportunities to share the process of discovery with their peers.

- Collaboration, an essential and valuable skill in school and in life, is discouraged.

- Students may have less opportunity to develop their communication and critical thinking skills.

Student Centered Learning

In student centred learning, the teacher is still the classroom authority figure. However, they function as more of a coach or facilitator while students embrace a more active and collaborative role in their own learning.

A student centred learning environment might look like one in which:

- The focus is shared by both the students and their teacher

- Students may have some choice in the topics they cover

- The instructor models a concept or challenge, then invites the students to explain or demonstrate it back to the class

- The students interact with their teacher and one another during the lesson

- Topics are delivered in familiar, everyday language students might use themselves; new vocabulary might get its own lesson

- Students work in pairs, in groups or alone depending on the activity

- The instructor refrains from constant monitoring but provides feedback or corrections when questions arise

- Students attempt to answer each other's questions, using their teacher as an information resource or facilitator

- Students evaluate their own learning alongside the teacher/instructor

- The classroom is busy and filled with energy

A student centred classroom may possess some or all of these qualities and may not work for every learning scenario. Some teachers and students may find student centred learning too chaotic, but testing out a healthy mix of teacher centred and student centred methods may be the key to success.

Benefits of a student centred Classroom

- Education becomes a more shared experience between the instructor and the students, and between the students themselves.

- Students build both collaboration and communication skills.

- Students tend to be more interested in learning when they can interact with one another and participate actively in their own education.

- Students learn to both work independently and to interact with others as part of the learning process.

Drawbacks of a student centred Classroom

- With students free to interact, the classroom space can feel noisy or chaotic.

- Classroom management can become more of an issue for the teacher, possibly cutting into instructional activities.

- With less focus on lectures, there can be a concern that some students may miss important information.

- Though collaboration is considered beneficial, this approach may not feel ideal for students who prefer to work alone.

- Some students may have difficulty focusing or retaining information in a collaborative, interactive setting.

Activity based Learning

Activity Based Learning is an instructional approach where students engage in activities directly related to the subject matter.

Instead of being mere recipients of information, they actively construct knowledge by doing tasks, participating in hands-on experiences, and being involved in real-life scenarios.

It is founded on the belief that learners learn best when they are actively involved in their education.

Steps of Activity-Based Learning

1. **Planning:** Identify clear learning objectives and plan activities around them.

2. **Engagement:** Start with an introductory activity to gauge students' prior knowledge and capture their interest.

3. **Execution:** Incorporate a variety of types of activity-based learning – from projects to games, ensuring all learning styles are catered to.

4. **Feedback:** After each activity, facilitate a feedback session. It allows for reflection and deeper understanding.

5. **Assessment:** Evaluate not just the end result, but also the process, collaboration, and individual contribution. Use

various digital assessment tools to help you in the evaluation of this part.

Skills Need for Teachers to Activity Based Learning

- **Creativity:** To design unique, engaging, and relevant activities.

- **Flexibility:** Teachers need to be ready to adapt if an activity isn't working as intended.

- **Observational Skills:** To monitor student participation, identify areas of struggle, and provide timely intervention.

- **Collaborative Spirit:** To work with fellow educators or industry experts, bringing richer experiences to students.

- **Continuous Learning:** As the types of activity-based learning evolve, so must the educator's skills and knowledge.

Challenges for Teachers to Activity Based Learning

- **Resource Intensive:** It might require specialized tools or materials which can be expensive or hard to source.

- **Time Consuming:** Planning and executing ABL can be more time-intensive than traditional lectures.

- **Classroom Management:** With students actively engaged in various tasks, it might get chaotic unless managed efficiently.

- **Assessment Difficulties:** Assessing group activities and hands-on tasks can be more challenging than grading a standard test.

- **Resistance to Change:** Both educators and students accustomed to traditional methods might find it hard to adapt.

Characteristics of Activity Based Learning:

1. **Active Student Participation:** Unlike traditional rote learning, ABL emphasizes active participation. Students engage in discussions, projects, and group work, ensuring they are always "doing" rather than just "listening."

2. **Real world Context:** Activity Based Learning incorporates real world situations into lessons. When students see how their learning applies outside of the classroom, it becomes more meaningful and relevant.

3. **Flexibility:** One of the most notable characteristics of Activity Based Learning is its flexibility. Lessons can be tailored to suit different learning styles and paces, allowing students to progress at a rate that's comfortable for them. This also covers students with special needs as online assessment software allows them to be on the same page as others.

4. **Collaboration:** This method often encourages group work. This not only promotes team-building but also enhances problem-solving skills and fosters a sense of community.

Types of Activity Based Learning:

There are various types of activity-based learning, each bringing its unique flair to the education table.

1. **Project-Based Learning:** This type of Activity Based Learning sees students undertaking larger projects that might span several weeks or even months. Whether it's creating a business plan or developing a community service project, students are deeply involved from conception to completion.

2. **Problem-Based Learning:** Here, students are presented with real world problems to solve. This method nurtures critical thinking, and students often utilize a multidisciplinary approach.

3. **Case-Based Learning:** This involves students analyzing real or fictional cases to derive solutions. It's a favourite in business and law disciplines.

4. **Game-Based Learning:** Who said learning can't be fun? By turning educational content into games, students become more engaged and might not even realize they're learning.

5. **Experiential Learning:** This encapsulates hands-on experiences, such as internships, field trips, or labs. I recall my own time as a student, where a trip to a local museum made history feel so much more tangible and alive than any textbook ever could.

3.2 Methods of Teaching

Inductive method

Think of the inductive method of teaching as flipping the coin on the usual classroom scene. Usually, you start with the theories or principles and then maybe show an example.

But when it comes to the inductive method, you start with examples, data, and observations. It's like putting together a puzzle: Students examine individual pieces (observations) and work their way toward seeing the whole picture (theories or principles).

In simpler terms, the inductive method of teaching lets students learn by doing. They observe, they question, and through these experiences, they uncover the big ideas on their own. It's all about discovery.

Steps of Inductive Method of Teaching

This kind of teaching method involves a systematic process that empowers students to construct knowledge through active engagement. Let's explore the key steps involved in this approach, allowing students to delve into the subject matter and develop their insights.

1. Introduce Relevant Learning Materials: To kick-start this method, teachers provide students with various learning materials, such as examples, images, keywords, or data.

2. Encourage Familiarity: Students are asked to seek familiarity within the provided materials. They actively search for elements they can relate to, connecting their existing knowledge with the new information at hand.

3. Identify Patterns: Instructing students to identify patterns is a crucial aspect of this method. By carefully examining the materials, students begin recognizing recurring elements or relationships.

4. Problem Identification: Building on the patterns identified, students are guided to identify a problem or issue that requires resolution.

5. Generate and Evaluate Solutions: Students are encouraged to generate various potential solutions to the identified problem. By brainstorming and considering various approaches, they engage in divergent thinking. Subsequently, they evaluate the feasibility and effectiveness of each solution, aiming to select the best course of action.

6. Organize Steps and Formulate Conclusions: In this final step, students organize the necessary steps to complete the task or solve the problem. They critically analyse the information gathered, draw logical conclusions, and formulate a hypothesis or generalization based on their findings.

Advantages of Inductive Method of Teaching

1. Active Learning: Inductive method of teaching encourages active student participation, fostering deeper engagement and comprehension.

2. Critical Thinking: Students enhance their critical thinking and problem-solving skills by analyzing specific instances and drawing general conclusions.

3. Conceptual Understanding: Inductive method of teaching promotes a deeper understanding of concepts as students construct knowledge from concrete examples.

4. Student-Centered Approach: This method empowers students to take ownership of their learning, promoting autonomy and independence.

5. Application in Real-World Scenarios: This method prepares students to apply their knowledge and reasoning skills to real-world situations, enhancing their learning experience.

Disadvantages of Inductive Method of Teaching

While this method has numerous benefits, it is essential to consider its potential drawbacks:

1. Time-Consuming: The inductive approach requires time for students to explore examples, identify patterns, and develop generalizations, which may impact the overall pace of the curriculum.

2. Limited Structure: As students actively construct knowledge, some individuals may struggle with the lack of a rigid structure, requiring additional guidance from the teacher.

3. Potential Generalization Errors: Students may arrive at incorrect or incomplete generalizations if the examples provided are sufficient or accurate.

4. Varied Student Responses: The open-ended nature of this method can result in diverse student responses, making it challenging for teachers to address individual differences effectively.

Deductive Method of Teaching

Deductive method is the reverse of the inductive method. In this method rules, generalizations and principles are provided to find students and then they are asked to verify them with the help of particular examples: The teacher's work is much simplified by giving a rule and asking the pupils to verify it by application to several concrete examples.

Steps of Deductive Method of Teaching

This teaching method involves three general initiatives:

(i) Activity planning: In this, teachers determine the concept which needs to be taught to ensure that the point of the lesson is firmly driven home. It will help in covering all the important points without missing any.

(ii) Activity execution: This involves establishing a connection between the concepts that had been taught in the previous class and what will be taught at present. Teachers can ask students questions related to the previous class to gauge their understanding before proceeding further.

(iii) Activity evaluation: It includes asking questions to distinguish between concepts and questions related to individual topics taught so far. This can be in the form of multiple-choice questions for making a distinction or short-answer-type questions to be explained with relevant examples. It will help teachers in evaluating individual efforts of students. Anyone who missed a class can also be identified and special attention can be paid to him/her.

Advantages of the Deductive Method of Teaching

The benefits of deductive methodologies of teaching are as follows:

i.   Students solve problems more quickly and efficiently.

ii. It is easy to cover most of the materials through this method.

iii.   Quick learning is encouraged as it is a short and time-saving technique. While teaching mathematics, the solutions to problems require less time because of the pre-established formulae.

iv.   It is a more efficient method in the long run.

v.   Encourages students to memorize the rules and is beneficial for the 'practice and revision' stage.

vi.   The deficiencies of the inductive learning approach aren't present in this learning method.

Disadvantages of the Deductive Method of Teaching

Here are some disadvantages of this method:

i.   It is not fit for improving students' reasoning capabilities.

ii.   Sometimes beginners may find it tough to comprehend an abstract formula due to a lack of acquaintance with various concrete instances.

iii.   The technique needs students to blindly memorize a lot of formulae, which might make them feel overwhelmed. Because of this, they often tend to forget the formulae. Inability to recollect them during an exam renders all efforts futile.

iv.   Eventually, memory is prioritized over understanding and intelligence in this technique, which is educationally unsound.

Difference between inductive and deductive teaching

Aspect	Inductive Teaching	Deductive Teaching
Approach	General statements generated from specific observations. For example: If the teacher has to differentiate between terrestrial, aerial and aquatic animals, she will show the students a picture of each kind like a cat, a crow and a fish. After that she will ask the students to figure out similar animals.	Particular statements generated from general observations. For example : In this case, the teacher will first explain the characteristics of terrestrial, aerial and aquatic animals and then give examples of each like a cat, a crow and a fish.
Learner Engagement	Students actively discover and explore material on their own.	Students receive information through lectures or instruction.
Suitable for	Often used with children and in informal settings.	Commonly used in structured academic environments.
Learning Experience	Experiment-like approach where students engage in discovery.	Lecture-style approach where students receive information.
Teacher's Role	Facilitator, guiding students in the process of discovery.	Instructor, providing information and guiding understanding.
Critical Thinking	Encourages critical thinking and problem-solving skills.	Provides opportunities for logical reasoning and analysis.
Knowledge Acquisition	Students construct knowledge based on personal exploration.	Students receive knowledge from the teacher or textbooks.

Flexibility	Allows for flexibility and adaptability in the learning process.	Follows a more structured and predetermined approach.
Application	Well-suited for fostering creativity and independent thinking.	Emphasizes the transmission of established knowledge.

To summarize the above, this method promotes active learning, discovery, and critical thinking, making it ideal for encouraging creativity and independent thinking. On the other hand, deductive teaching involves a more structured approach focusing on imparting established knowledge to students. Both methods have unique advantages and applications, and educators may choose the most appropriate approach based on the learning objectives and the needs of the learners.

Lecture cum demonstration Method of Teaching

It is one of Traditional method. This is also known as Chalk and talk method. Teacher cantered method. In this method Teacher is active and learners are passive. The essentials qualities in learning science such as independent thinking, power of observation and reasoning can be developed in this method. Demonstration method is a teacher- centred method as the teacher demonstrates the pictures/ charts/models/experiments and explains the principles, concepts involved in these demonstrated materials or processes. The students observe the demonstration shown by the teacher and some of them participate in answering the questions asked by the teacher and draw conclusions.

Criteria of a good lecture - demonstration method

> The demonstration should be planned and rehearsed well in advance. Planning and rehearsing of the experiment is very essential for it gives confidence in the demonstrator. he find out the difficulties involved in the experiment. So that the lesson will go smoothly and systematically.

> The teacher should be clear of the purpose of demonstration. He should know the aims and objectives of the demonstration.

> Demonstration should be the result of the active participation of pupils and teacher. Teacher helps the students in arranging and fitting and performing the experiment.

Characteristics of good demonstration:

> Visibility

> One major idea at a time

> Clear cut

> Convincing

> Rehearsal

> Supplemented with other teaching aids

> Asking relevant questions

> Neat, clean and tidiness

> Simple and speedy

> To write observation

➢ Teacher to act as performer

➢ Sufficient time

Steps involved in the demonstration method:

a. Planning

b. Introduction

c. Demonstration

d. Blackboard usage

e. Concepts compilation

Planning:

1. Ensure whether the lesson is suitable for this method.
2. Collect necessary tools, equipments, and materials for demonstration.
3. Rehearse the experiment before demonstrating before the class as it will help to build confidence to demonstrate.
4. Be ready with explanatory notes and questions to be used during and after the demonstration.

Introduction:

1. Motivate the students to arouse interest in observing the experiment keenly and to accept new concepts after the demonstration.
2. Introduce the lesson as a 'problem' or an issue, so that the students understand the importance of the lesson.

Demonstration:

1. Keep the curiosity of the students alive during the demonstration.
2. Take care to ensure that the students are able to follow the demonstration.
3. Relate the demonstration with the life experiences of the students.
4. Handle the instruments safely, and arrange them in their respective places for the demonstration.

Blackboard Usage:

1. Write the objectives clearly on the black board to make the students understand the significance of the demonstration method.
2. Draw relevant pictures and write the key concepts and the results of the demonstration immediately on the black board.
3. Ask the students to write the key points, draw the diagram and finally the results in their notebooks.
4. Check their notebooks while they are writing.

Besides the above mentioned points, you need to take care of the following aspects:

➢ Do tell the purpose of the demonstration to the students but do not tell the inferences or conclusions in advance.

➤ Seek the help of students in arranging, and performing the experiment. Quality of demonstration is better when you along with your students actively participate in it.

➤ Be well versed in the handling of apparatus and arrange those for the demonstration in a definite order which the students can clearly observe.

➤ Check that the demonstration is clearly visible to all students in the class.

➤ Ensure that the demonstration is simple and according to the mental level of the students.

➤ Supplement the demonstration with other teaching aids to make it more real and interesting.

Advantages:

➤ Save time and money.

➤ Student participation.

➤ Helpful to promote useful discussion.

➤ More efficient method

➤ Activity method

➤ Helpful for teacher

Disadvantages:

> - Visibility: Visibility is main problem for a teacher because all the students may not be able to see the details and results of a demonstration.

> - Speed of experiment: Either too fast or too slow speed of demonstration sometimes may create trouble.

> - Ignorance of individual difference.

> - This method somehow hinders the development of laboratory skills among the students.

> - Not useful for developing scientific attitude

Laboratory Method of Teaching

This method in commonly thought of as a hands on and minds on approach to teach science where in students have the opportunity to gain some experience with phenomena associated with their course of study. In this method either student participate alone or in small groups. They produce or manipulate various variables that are under exploration. The degree to which student has control over exploration can vary over a wide range. Here the students learn by actual doing rather than my observing the experiments. As young children do it by themselves, the experience is impressed more firmly in their minds. Thus this method in psychologically sound as it satisfies the natural urge for activity. This method broadens interest of the students. They learn many virtues through laboratory activity. The experience in a laboratory is very rich in personal satisfaction as they gain it firsthand. The sense of excitement and challenge help them to achieve some tangible him.

Principles of laboratory method

1. It follows the principle of learning by doing.

2. It follows psychological principle, where students age, lord and interest is taken into consideration.

3. The work should be Pre-organized and Pre-selected.

4. Teacher must see that, students are allowed to work independently without much interference.

5. The teacher must ensure that apparatus and equipments should be checked pair hand.

6. Teacher must see that students are able to follow in struction and record their observation properly.

Role of teacher

1. Teacher must be a facilitator of the process of doing experiments by students.

2. Teacher must check the apparatus previously, so that it goes on smoothly.

3. The practical work must be Pre-organized and Pre-selected.

4. The skills of handling apparatus, drawing, diagrams, careful observations taking necessary precautions, must be developed among students.

5. The teacher must be that, the student is doing experiment properly by following proper procedure.

Merits of laboratory method

1. This method follows child-centered approach.

2. It makes students active and alert.

3. It gives scope for learning by doing and students do a lot of thinking themselves.

4. Different skills are developed.

5. It paves way for exploration experimentation and verification of scientific facts and principles.

6. It inculcates good virtues like, honesty, truthfulness, dignity of labour etc.

7. It helps in developing sprit of enquiring.

8. It helps in developing higher order this king capacities like reasoning, analyzing, synthesizing etc.

Limitations of laboratory method

1. It is expensive and uneconomical.

2. It is time consuming as it takes much time in some experiments to come to conclusion.

3. It expects a lot from students and teacher.

4. It does not guarantee that, students would be equally efficient in solving problems outside laboratory.

5. All students cannot be expected to be skilled workers.

6. Most of the students are either not ready or lack to ability to undertake original work.

Suggestions to improve

1. This method should not be considered independently but should form a part of the total science programme.

2. The practical work must be pre-planned.

3. It is imperative that same individual laboratory work must be done by every student.

4. Instead of performing the experiments started in the book should be little modified for better result.

5. Before experiment in performed the purpose must be clarified to the students.

Project Method of Teaching

The project method is an alternative classroom model that gives more focus on the aspect of student learning rather than the teaching aspect of the lesson. It emphasizes trusting the students and not imposing a learning style onto them. The responsibility of the work falls directly on the students since even the curriculum content and technique is considered from the student's POV. So this method is completely student-centric. This method is based on the philosophy of Pragmatism and the principle of 'Learning by doing'. The project method is a teacher facilitated collaborative approach in which students acquire and apply knowledge and skills to define and solve realistic problems using a process of extended inquiry

The project method of teaching is generally considered to have been formulated, developed, executed, and perfected by educator William H. Kilpatrick. Even though it is deemed to have been proposed as a concept back in 1908 as a means of improving the method of teaching agriculture, Kilpatrick is credited with elaborating upon the concept and popularizingit worldwide in his famous article, "The Project Method" which was published in 1918.

According to W.H. Kilpatrick - A project is a whole- hearted purposeful activity proceeding in a social environment.

According to Ballord - A project is a bit of real life that has been imparted into school.

According to Stevenson - Project is a problematic act carried to completion in its natural setting.

According to Thomas & Long - It is a voluntary undertaking which involves constructive effort or thought and eventuates into objective results.

Characteristics of project method

- It takes the student beyond the walls of the class room.

- It is carried out in a natural setting, thus making learning realistic and experiential.

- It encourages investigative learning and solution of practical problems.

- It is focused on the student as it enlists his/her active involvement in the task set.

- It encourages the spirit of scientific enquiry as it involves validation of on evidence hypotheses based gathered from the investigation.

- It promotes a better knowledge of the practical aspects of knowledge gained from books.

- It enhances the student's social skills, requires as it interaction with the social environment.

- Teacher plays a facilitative role rather than the role of an expert.

- It allows the students a great degree of freedom to choose from among the options given to them; hence it provides a psychological boost.

- It encourages the spirit of research in the student.

Project Method - 5 Steps

Creating Situation: Teacher creates the proper situation to the students in the class. Puts up the knowledge about the project method procedure, steps, and uses to the students. It should never be forced on them. It should be purposeful and significant.

Project Selection: Select project work, Students choose problem with most utility & practical need, teachers guide & motivate based on aptitude.

Planning: Planning phase, teacher guides students, facilitates discussion for views & suggestions, raises objections & related problems.

Execution: After planning, comes execution phase where students carry out project work as per plan, assigning duties based on interests and capabilities, and contributing individually towards completion through data collection, visits, information gathering, reading history etc. Teacher guides and provides necessary information.

Evaluation: The fifth and final stage of the project method is evaluation. The whole work is reviewed by the teacher and students get judged or assessed on the basis of their performance. They carry out the project as planned, following which the mistakes they have made in the process are noted down.

Reporting and Recording: It is the last step of the project method in which each and every step of the work is reported. The reported things are recorded in a certain order in a book form. It should include the proposal, plan and its discussion, duties allotted to different students and how far they were carried out by them. It should also include the details of places visited and surveyed guidance for future and all other possible details. The book formatted report is submitted to the teacher at the end.

Types of Project Method of Teaching

The proponent of Project Method, Kilpatric, classified it in his book "Foundation of Method" into four types:

1. Constructive project: Practical or physical tasks such as constructions of article, making a model are done in this type of projects.

2. Aesthetic project: Appreciation powers of the students are developed in this type of project through the musical programmes, beautification of something, appreciation of poems and so on.

3. Problematic project: In this type of project develops the problem solving capacity of the students through their experiences. It is based on the cognitive domain.

4. Drill project: It is for the mastery of the skill and knowledge of the students. It increases the work efficacy and capacity of the students.

Role of the teacher

➢ In project method of teaching the role of a teacher is that of a guide, friend and philosopher.

➤ The teacher is not a dictator or a commander but a friend, guide and a working partner. He encourages his students to work collectively, and co-operatively.

➤ He also helps his students to avoid mistakes.

➤ He makes it a point that each member of the group contributed somethingto the completion of the project.

➤ If the students face failure during execution of some steps of the project the teacher should not execute any portion of the project but should suggest them some better methods of techniques that may be used by them next time for the success of the project.

➤ He should help the students in developing the character and personality by allowing them to accept the responsibilities and discharge them efficiently.

➤ He should provide democratic atmosphere in the class so that the pupils can express themselves fully without any fear of the teacher.

➤ He should be alert and active all the time to see that the project is running in its right lines.

➤ He should have a thorough knowledge of individual children so as to allot them work accordingly.

➤ He should have initiative, tact and zest for learning.

- ➢ Teacher should always remain alert and active during execution step and see that the project goes to completion successfully.

- ➢ During execution of the project teacher should maintain a democratic atmosphere.

- ➢ Teacher must be well read and wellinformed so that he can help the students to the successful completion of the project.

Types of project

1. Individual and Social (Group) projects: In individual projects, every student solves the problem in their own according to their interest, capacity, attitude and needs. It develops the problem solving qualities individually and not the social qualities.

2. In Social (Group) projects: In Social projects the problem is solved by the group of pupil in the class. Here the social, citizenship qualities and synergism are develops.

3. Simple and Complex project: Simple and Complex project In the simple projects the students are completing only one work at a time. It gives the deep information about the project in a one angle. The students get deeper and broader knowledge about the problem.

4. Complex project: In the complex project the students are carried out more than one work at a time. They are focuses on the work in various subject and angles. Here the students get the knowledge about the work in various activities and dimensions.

Advantages of Project Method:

- ➢ **Active Learning Experience:** The project method emphasizes the concept of learning by doing. Enhancing their skillset, first-hand experiences, and thinking capacity.

- ➢ **Inculcating a Sense of Responsibility:** In the project method of teaching, the teacher is a guide and the activities carried out in the class are carried out by the students themselves. This helps improve self-reliance and self-responsibility among students.

- ➢ **Improves Collaboration Among Students:** Project-based learning helps students work together, fostering professional and personal bonds that make the learning experience enjoyable and enlightening. It encourages cooperation, developing social skills.

- ➢ **Improves Communication Skills:** It helps students improve their communicative skills drastically because students are given the opportunity to express themselves freely among their peers as well as their teachers, hence helping them communicate more effectively.

- ➢ **Improves Critical Thinking Skills:** Critical thinking skills are 21st Century Skills that students of all ages need to have in today's time. It is something that needs to be cultivated with respect to the future of the students and needs to be dealt with with utmost diligence.

Disadvantages of Project Method of Teaching:

> ➤ **Time Consuming:** Teaching students using the project method can be time consuming as there are a lot of things that need to be taken into consideration when teaching using this method such as the student's ability to comprehend the subject, the speed with which they do so, the factual accuracy of the project and so on. There are a lot of factors that need to be observed and duly corrected by the teacher. This is the perfect segue into the next point: the lack of expert teachers.

> ➤ **The Lack of Experienced Teachers:** The project method of teaching can only be conducted by experienced teachers who have several years of experience, which a lot of teachers may not have. This leads to a shortage of teachers and hence incapability to execute this form of teaching effectively.

> ➤ **Not Suitable for All Subjects:** The project method of teaching is most suitable for subjects that require practical knowledge and so subjects such as arts, literature and so on may not benefit a lot from this form of teaching.

Problem Solving Method of Teaching

The problem-solving method is a highly effective teaching strategy that is designed to help students develop critical thinking skills and problem solving abilities. It involves providing students with real-world problems and challenges that require them to apply their knowledge, skills, and creativity to find solutions. This method encourages active learning, promotes collaboration, and allows students to take ownership of their learning. Problem-solving is a process of identifying, analyzing, and resolving problems.

According to Skinner - Problem solving is the process of overcoming difficulties that hinder the achievement of a goal.

According to John Dewey - Problem solving is woven into the fabric of logical thinking. The problem determines the goal and the goal controls the thinking process.

Skills use in problem solving

> Planning

> Critical thinking skills

> Analytical skills

> Collecting information

> Decision making

Purpose of problem solving method

> Train the students in the act of reasoning.

> Gain and improve the knowledge

> Solve puzzling question

> Overcome the obstacles in the attainment of objectives.

Steps of problem solving

Following are the steps in this method:

1. Define the Problem: The first step in problem-solving is to clearly define the problem at hand. Take the time to understand the root cause, identify the desired outcome, and gather relevant information. This step sets the foundation for the entire problem-solving process.

2. Analyse the Situation: Once the problem is defined, it's important to analyze the situation thoroughly. Break down the problem into smaller components, examine any patterns or trends, and consider any constraints or limitations. This analysis will help you gain a deeper understanding of the problem and its underlying factors.

3. Generate Possible Solutions: With a clear understanding of the problem, it's time to brainstorm potential solutions. Encourage creativity and consider all possible options, even if they seem unconventional. This step is about quantity, not quality, so aim to generate as many ideas as possible.

4. Evaluate and Select the Best Solution: After generating a list of potential solutions, it's time to evaluate each option based on its feasibility, effectiveness, and alignment with the desired outcome. Consider the pros and cons of each solution and weigh them against each other. Select the solution that appears to be the most viable and likely to solve the problem effectively.

5. Implement the Solution: Once you have chosen the best solution, it's time to put it into action. Develop a detailed plan, allocate necessary resources, and communicate the plan to relevant stakeholders. Ensure that everyone involved understands their roles and responsibilities in implementing the solution.

6. Monitor and Evaluate: Implementing the solution is not the end of the problem-solving process. Continuously monitor the progress and evaluate the effectiveness of the solution. If necessary, make adjustments or modifications to improve the outcome. Learning from the process is crucial for future problem-solving endeavors.

Features of the problem/ criteria for problem selection:

1. The problem should be meaningful, interesting, and worthwhile for children.

2. It should have some correlation with life.

3. It should have some correlation with other subjects if possible.

4. It should arise out of the real needs of the students.

5. The problem should be clearly defined.

6. The solution of problem should be found out by the student themselves working under the guidance and supervision of the teacher.

7. The problem should be intellectually challenging to children..

8. The problem should not be entirely unfamiliar to the learners

9. The problem should be related to their previous experience.

10. The problem should have practical relevance.

11. The problem should have the potential to create interest among in the specific problem in particular and problem solving in general.

Teacher role in problem solving

> Help the students to define the problem clearly. Got them to make many suggestions by encouraging them.

> To analyse the situation in parts.

> To recall previously known similar cases and general rules those apply

> To guess courageously and formulate guesses clearly. Get them to evaluate each suggestion carefully by encouraging them:

> To maintain a state of doubt or suspended conclusion.

> To criticize the suggestion by appeal to know facts minister and experiment Get them to organize the material by proceeding:

> To build an outline on the board To use diagrams and graphs

> To formulate concise statement of the net out -come of discussion.

Merits

1. It serves as a preparation for adult life.

2. It develops the power of critical thinking.

3. It makes pupil active recipient of knowledge.

4. It develops values of tolerance and open mindedness.

5. It helps for the easy assimilation of knowledge.

6. It is a general procedure in finding solutions to daily occurrences that urgently need to be addressed.

7. The students become appreciative and grateful for the achievement of scientists.

8. Critical thinking, open-mindedness and wise judgment are among scientific attitudes and values inculcated through competence in the scientific method.

9. The students learn to accept the opinions and evidence shared by others.

Demerits

1. This method will become monotonous if used to frequently.

2. The problem solving method can easily lead to the selection of trivial and untimely topics.

3. This is appropriate for developing cognitive competencies, but not for bringing about affective changes.

4. Generally speaking problem – solving involves mental activity only.

5. Small children do not posses sufficient background information& therefore they fail to participation in discussion.

6. Students may not have adequate reference and sources books.

7. It need very capable teacher to provide effective guidance and knowledge to students.

8. It is a time consuming process, teacher may find it difficult to complete the syllabus.

3.3 Self-instructional techniques: Programmed learning (Linear and Branched), Computer Assisted Instruction (CAI)

Instructional techniques are concerned with bringing improvement in the effectiveness and efficiency of learning in the educational context. Every teaching becomes effective when it focuses on utilization of different instructional techniques to facilitate learners' growth and development from all aspects.

Self-Instructional Materials (SIM) is a type of instructional material that enables learners to acquire knowledge and skills in a self-paced, self-directed manner. SIM is designed to provide learners with a flexible and accessible learning experience that allows them to take control of their learning process.

Programmed learning

The programmed instruction method is a highly individualised instructional new strategy for the modification of teacher behaviour. Though used for instructional purposes it can also be employed as a mechanism of feedback device for improving teaching efficiency. Its theoretical knowledge is essential to use for the modification of teacher behaviour. It is in fact a strategy in which various kinds of intellectual, emotional and motor experiences are provided to the learner in a controlled situation. This technique of instruction was basically developed by B.F.Skinner. This technique is fundamentally based on the principle of reinforcement and self-learning, i.e., based on the theory of trial and error and operant conditioning. This is a technique of learning in which the learner goes forward himself in the process of learning. Thus, it has contributed a lot in reducing the load of a teacher in formal education system.

Meaning

"Programming refers to the arrangement of the stimulus material in an order of presentation that would maximise the rate of learning, resulting in optimal behaviour modification on the prescribed lines."

In this method the material to be learned is arranged in graded units, according to the level of difficulty. It is presented in such an order that it results in the best understanding and retention. Thus a programme is the subject matter to be learned by the students, while programming is the new method of arranging the subject matter to be picked up by the pupils, in graded steps arranged in a psychological and logical sequence having its meaning dependant on the principles of 'from concrete to abstract' and from 'familiar to new'. Here the pupil proceeds from 'fact' to a 'concept'.

Here the learner's responses are gradually shaped to the desired level or refinement. The origin of programming may be credited to Sidney Pressey (1920s) who developed a series of mechanical devices which aims at presenting multiple choice questions to the learners after instruction and which gave them immediate answers. It is based on the principle of reinforcement. This method of teaching is an autocratic and individualised strategy. It is based on the psychological principles of operant condition. The responses of the learner are strictly controlled by the programmer. Its main focus is to bring desirable change in the cognitive domain of the learner's behaviour. The structure of teaching method is that the selected content is analysed and broken into smaller elements. Each element is independent and complete in itself. The programmer develops frames based on each element. Responses are also provided to the learner in the program on some different leaflets. The correct response of the learner is the new knowledge or new behaviour. Immediate confirmation of correct response provides reinforcement to the learner and he proceeds to the next frame. Wrong responses required feedback. Physical presence of the teacher is not necessary. He may come to give instructions regarding the program. Students are left for learning at their pace. Thus, even in the absence of a teacher, the work of teaching can proceed profitably. The programmes can be made available in the form of books, cards or machines.

Definitions

Programmed instruction has been defined as a method of giving individualized instruction, in which the student is active and proceeds at his own pace and is provided with immediate knowledge of result. The physical presence of the teacher is not essential in this strategy.

Sussan Markle (1969) gave a wider definition of programmed instruction. "It is a method of designing a reproducible sequence of instructional events to produce a measurable and consistent effect on behaviour of each and every acceptable student." Smith and Moore(1962) " Programmed instruction is the process of arranging the material to be learned into a series of sequential steps, usually it moves the student from familiar background to a complex and new set of concepts, principles and understanding.

Michael J Apter "Programmed instruction is a method of instruction in which the information to be taught is broken down into small units which are to be presented to the student (usually in written form) in a carefully planned sequence. Each unit or 'frame' contains not only information but is also terminated with a question.

Principles of Programme Instruction

The basic principles of programmed instruction are as follows:

1. Principle of small steps

2. Principle of active responding

3. Principle of feedback

4. Principle of self-pacing

5. Principle of error control

1. Principle of small steps: This principle includes an analysis of content/subject matter to be learned or taught. The subject or skill to be acquired is broken into small steps. Learning takes place most rapidly if the subject matter is presented in small steps so that the success of the student on the new item is ensured. Each step known as a frame is presented to the student at a time. All the steps are arranged in a logical sequence. Thus, the student proceeds step by step (frame by frame) and achieves the terminal objective put before him or her. Learning each frame gives the student a feeling of satisfaction which in turn reinforces his learning.

2. Principle of active responding: Another principle of programmed instruction is based on active responding by the students. Learners are made to interact with every bit of information and make a response, because the assumption underlying this principle is that in order for meaningful learning to occur, a response must be made by the learner, and the learner should be actively engaged with the subject matter. Responses may be overt (when learners write the answers) or covert (when learners think out the answers).

3. Principle of feedback: The term feedback means 'knowledge of results'. Experimental evidence supports this principle that the more immediate, the reward better is the learning. The student comes to know immediately whether he is on the right track. Learning accompanied with success or satisfaction is likely to be more permanent than learning accompanied by failure or dissatisfaction. This mechanism is known as 'controlling the behaviour of the student'.

4. Principle of self-pacing: Programmed instruction is based on the assumption that the individual student learns according to his own pace, needs and capabilities. It is student-centred and encourages each student to work at his own speed. Individualised instruction is brought about through self-paced workbooks, branching/scrambled books.

5. Principle of error control: Programmed instruction is closely linked to the issue of error control. The learning sequence is broken down into a large number of small steps, so that the rate of error is kept down to a minimum and allows reinforcement to be frequent and immediate. Formative evaluation of the programme helps to reduce errors to a minimum. Thus, it helps to concentrate more on analysis of student performance rather than on his errors.

Characteristics of Programmed Instruction

1. It is a part of educational technology in the sense that programmed material can be presented with the help of machines or computers.

2. It is a new strategy of teaching and learning. Here, learner learns himself without the help of the teacher. Thus, the problem of the dearth of effective teachers can be overcome.

3. It is a technique for the solution of educational as well as teaching problems. We can supply programmed instructional materials to lakhs of students at a time and can help them to have access to the latest knowledge and its dimensions.

4. It is a technique for the modification of learner's behaviour. Thus, it is opposite of micro teaching where teacher's behaviour is modified. Learner's behaviour is modified by confirming the right response immediately.

5. It cannot replace the teacher from the field of teaching altogether. It is because only an effective teacher can prepare a good programmed material.

6. It requires more creativity and imaginative efforts to develop such individualized instructional material. Every individual learner learns at his own speed here.

Steps of preparation of a Programme Instruction

Preparation of programmed instruction text involves three stages:

Stage -1: Preparation

Stage-2: Writing the Frames

Stage-3: Evaluation or Try out / revision

STAGE 1: Preparation Stage: This stage is also known as the planning stage. The teacher selects the topic for the programme. He should be thoroughly familiar with the topic and limit the area to be dealt and decide the suitability of the programme. He should identify the objectives and then do the content analysis for developing the instructional procedure. Writing objectives here means keeping clear the entering behaviour and the terminal behaviour which the programme intends to bring about. Developing the criterion test for assessing the performance acquired in the programmed and to evaluate the attainment of the objectives is also done. Here identifying the entering behaviour describes the abilities and skills which are essential for the instructions leading to new terminal behaviour.

STAGE 2: Writing the Frames: This stage involves designing of the frames, sequencing of the frames and editing of the programmes. Designing the frame needs to fulfilled four components, viz, the stimulus, the response, prompts or cues and confirmation of results. The stimulus is a small segment of content that is presented in a frame. The format of response is generally a blank. This stimulus material of the frame and the response constitutes an S-R relationship. Immediate confirmation of results is provided and the correct response is usually given against the next frame. The student compares his response with the given one and if he is correct he moves ahead. Prompt is a supplementary stimulus which is added to the terminal stimulus to make the item easier. It helps the student to give correct response and prevents him from making unnecessary errors.

STAGE 3: Evaluation or try out/revision: This is the last stage of the development of the programme. It helps the programmer to assess whether the programme is an effective instructional tool or not. When the first draft is ready, it should be tried out on several persons and re-edited. The original frames should be typed and their response given on the back page. Now it should be given to small group of students. It has to be seen where mistakes are being committed. This will facilitate revision of the frames later. Two types of evaluation are conducted - the internal and external evaluation.

STYLES OF PROGRAMMING Programmed instruction was introduced in the 1950s in classroom teaching and since then many styles of programming have emerged. The three main types which we will be discussing here are as follows:

a) Linear programming style

b) Branching programming style

c) Mathetics

a) Linear programming style: A linear programme consists of a series of small segments of instructional units called frames. Subject matter is presented to a student in small bits. In this style of programming, all students proceed in a predetermined way, i.e., all students follow the same linear sequence of frames, each frame being of small size. The student starts from the initial frame and progresses towards the terminal frame. As the sequence is linear and every student follows an identical path decided by the programmer, so linear programmes are considered to be extrinsic. Linear programme allows students to progress at their own rate through a series of small steps, each step proceeding logically through the subject matter. The students begin with frame one and then proceed to frame two. Each box represents a frame.

b) Branching programming style: Branching style of programming was conceived by a psychologist, Norman Crowder in 1954 and it is also called as the Crowderian style of programming and has been defined as a programme which adapts to the needs of the students without the medium of extrinsic device such as computer. This style of programming is also called intrinsic because herein the learner within himself makes the decision to adapt the instruction to his needs according to his background of the subject. In this programming, a student is to read a unit of material followed by a multiple choice question. If he chooses the right answer to the next question, he is presented the next paragraph of the material and the next question. If he chooses the wrong response, then he is presented the material, written specifically to rectify his errors. This remedial material is followed by a direction to return to the original presentation to make a second choice. Thus the student proceeds through programmes along different routes or branches.

c) Mathetics: The word Mathetics is derived from the Greek word 'mathein' which means 'to learn'. This style of programming was first conceived by Thomas Gilbert in 1962 and is defined as 'the systematic application of reinforcement theory to the analysis and reconstruction of those complex behaviour repertoires usually known as subject matter mastery of knowledge and skills.' Mathetics tends to use much larger frames to maximize step size and produces frames with as few frames as possible. Gilbert called the step/frame an exercise. The mathetics exercises are presented on various logical techniques for structuring the subject matter. The main objective is that student is supposed to do the exercises and master that particular operation/task. It is a prescriptive rather than descriptive process.

Advantages of Programmed Instruction

1. Student is kept active and alert: It makes the student active and self reliant. He gets good exercise in using new words, concepts and relationships; and lack of attention is detected immediately. Even if he commits a mistake, he is immediately aware of it and can correct himself. It is individualized learning and the student can proceed at his own pace.

2. Learning is made easy and simple: It makes learning easy and simple because the learning material is presented in small instalments due to individualized learning, it motivates the student for further learning.

3. Teacher gets relieved of doing ordinary jobs and he can play the role of guide, counsellor, motivator, organiser, etc. It may help the teacher in reduction of their total load of work. The time thus saved may be utilized by the teacher in some creative activities.

4. A well-programmed self-instructional device is tailored to cater to the needs of individual students of the class: It helps to yield good results as the programmes are better prepared and planned material. And it is better as compared to traditional teaching method. It gives self-motivation to the students. It also helps to do work in an organised and systematic manner without pressuring the students. And each student work at his own interest and pace.

5. Programmed instruction makes learning interesting: The learning material is presented in such a way that learning becomes an interesting game in which the learner is challenged by his capabilities. The novelty of learning by advice provides extra motivation to the learner. It develops scientific attitude among the learners because they are able to think rationally and logically.

6. Helpful for in-service teachers and correspondence studies: In-service teachers can be kept abreast with the latest developments in the field of education through programmed instruction material. It also quite useful for correspondence course students who want to continue their higher studies by sitting at home or by continuing studies along with their jobs or vocations.

7. Programmed instruction is helpful for teaching complex subject-matter: The complexity of the material is simplified through the analysis of the subject-matter into small and more easily assimilated segments of information. Well-programmed materials give the teacher the method and the individual sufficient time to comprehend more complex concepts.

8. Programmed Instructions, as a teaching procedure, is particularly useful for developing countries and where there is shortage of good teachers. It is very useful in certain situations where human instructors are not easy to provide, e.g., small isolated schools in the hilly areas.

9. Failing standards can be easily checked and suitable remedial measures can be given with the help of programmed material. And for those few, who are intelligent or gifted, they can be provided with more courses through programme instructions and thus they can make more progress without hindering the rest of the class.

Limitations

1. The orthodox teachers who are indifferent to any change in methodology of teaching will not relish accepting programmed learning material for classroom teaching.

2. Teacher taught relationship is important but through programmed learning it is not strengthened.

3. Some students are not habitual of working at their own and may not study at all. A few of them may become lazy and not want to proceed further.

4. There is a need for preparing suitable programmes for the learners in the Indian situations which is not possible and will be quite expensive too.

5. It cannot foster proper attitudes, aesthetic appreciation, moral standards, etc.

6. In programmed learning, subject matter is presented to the learners and they give response. It does not help in the development of their imagination.

7. No flexibility is there because every learner has to follow the same track rigidly.

8. This programme is totally proved to be worthless when the student's starts looking at the key without reading the frame and we do not have any mechanism to control this dishonest behaviour of the learners.

9. The preparation cost of this material is also very high. And it is also a time consuming method of learning and makes the students bored very soon.

Computer Assisted Instruction (CAI)

The computer assisted instruction is a system of teaching method regulated by the computer. Using computers as an important unit of teaching environment is called as computer assisted instruction.

Features of CAI

- Here computer create a creative environment for the purpose of imparting the knowledge.

- There are many programmes that facilitate learning.

- It helps learn in effective and meaningful way.

- It displays the education material in a modern way.

- Resources are provide individually and in as grouped.

- It provides the student to construct their own knowledge and to exercise on the subjects.

- It provides the exercises with games to make it more interesting and records the progress of the student by evaluation.

- It organizes the daily routine of the student with the series of teaching program.

- It provides records, marks and progress of the students for further verification.

- It helps the student to participate in the tutorial and interactive classes.

- It checks with the records of the students learning and decides programs as per his capacity.

- It also records the details of the students who have undergone the computer assisted instruction.

Modes of CAI

- Drill and Practice

- Tutorial

- Simulation

- Instructional Game

- Problem-Solving

- Other

Drill and Practice

- Exercises designed to increase fluency in a new skill or body of knowledge or to refresh an existing skill or body of knowledge.

- This approach assumes that the learners have previously been introduced to the content.

- Good programs provide user control, give feedback and reinforcement, and help learners master skills.

- Good for basic skills/knowledge where rapid student response is desired.

- Usually best to use in a series of brief sessions.

- Mainly intended for use by individuals.

- Should be geared to a level appropriate for the students.

Tutorial

- A form of CAI in which the computer assumes the role of a tutor - introducing content, providing practice, and assessing learning.

- Tutorials are used to introduce new content to learners in much the same manner that a human teacher might.

- Because tutorials present content to students, they can be used in any area of the curriculum for:

  - Remediation when learners lack necessary background knowledge.

  - Enrichment when learners wish to go beyond the basics.

  - Introduction of content to all learners (freeing the instructor to do other things).

- Good for verbal and conceptual learning.

- May require significant investment of students' time.

- Can be effectively used by individuals or groups of 2-3 students.

- Should be followed by opportunities for student application of knowledge.

Simulation

- A form of CAI that provides a simplified representation of a real situation, phenomenon, or process.

- Provides the opportunity for students to apply knowledge in a realistic format but without the time, expense, or risk associated with the real thing.

- Simulations can mimic physical objects or phenomena, processes, procedures, and situations.

- Best used for application of knowledge, problem solving and thinking skills.

- Time involvement may be brief or extended depending on the simulation.

- Good for small groups of students, although can be used by individuals.

- Often requires guidance and follow-up for effective use.

Instructional Game

- Usually another type of CAI (e.g., drill and practice or simulation) modified to include gaming elements.

- Generally features

    - an end goal and rules of play.

    - sensory appeal.

> – motivational elements (e.g., competition, cooperation, challenge, fantasy).

Problem-Solving

- CAI program that is designed to foster thinking or problem solving skills, but does not fit into one of the other categories.

- Usually focuses on a specific type of problem solving and provides practice on a number or variety of problems.

Other

- Many applications, particularly those that have been developed in recent years, are not easily classified into one of the preceding categories.

Advantages of Computer Assisted Instruction

- Computer through education is very effective because by using the computer we can show the pictures, videos, audios etc.

- It made a learning faster and meaning full.

- Complex subjects can be explain in simple & meaningful way.

- Example: the working of the heart can be explained shown by using the videos & animation

- It also help to self-learning: with the help of the videos and images we can try to learn all the times without the help of teacher.

- By using the computer, teacher can make the class room teaching interesting and different.

- By showing the variety of videos, Photos related to the topic to make teaching and learning process effective and easy

Disadvantages of Computer Assisted Instruction

- It is an expensive method.

- There is no scope for human or emotional aspects.

- It is too mechanical.

- It is not appropriate for students of all ages.

- It is not possible to assess the essay type questions.

- It is just difficult to learn all the subject through this method

3.4 Techniques- Augmented reality, virtual reality

Augmented reality (AR)

Augmented learning refers to the use of augmented reality (AR) technologies to enhance the learning experience. By integrating digital content with the physical world, augmented learning aims to create more interactive, engaging, and effective educational experiences. Here are some key aspects of augmented learning:

1. **Interactive Content**: AR can overlay interactive elements on physical objects or environments. For example, a student might point a tablet at a textbook, and AR could display 3D models or animations related to the text, helping to visualize complex concepts.

2. **Enhanced Engagement**: By integrating digital elements into the real world, AR can make learning more engaging and stimulating. This can be particularly beneficial for visual and kinesthetic learners who benefit from hands-on, immersive experiences.

3. **Real-World Context**: AR can provide contextual information related to physical objects or locations. For instance, in a science class, students could use AR to view the inner workings of a plant cell by scanning a real plant with their device.

4. **Gamification**: AR can incorporate game-like elements into learning, making it more enjoyable and motivating for students. This might include quizzes, challenges, or interactive simulations.

5. **Accessibility**: AR can provide additional resources and support, such as translations, definitions, or explanations,

making learning more accessible to students with diverse needs.

Overall, augmented learning leverages AR to make education more interactive, dynamic, and effective by bridging the gap between digital and physical worlds.

Virtual reality (VR)

Virtual reality (VR) is a technology that creates a simulated environment, allowing users to experience and interact with a computer-generated world as if it were real. This is usually achieved through a VR headset, which covers your eyes and sometimes includes headphones, to immerse you in a 360-degree environment. Some VR systems also include hand controllers or other sensors to track your movements and allow you to interact with the virtual world. VR is used in a variety of fields, including gaming, training, education, and even therapy.

Difference between Augmented reality and virtual reality

Particulars	Augmented Reality (AR)	Virtual Reality (VR)
Definition	AR overlays digital information (such as images, sounds, or data) onto the real world.	VR creates a completely immersive digital environment that replaces the real world.
Interaction	You can still see and interact with your physical environment while interacting with virtual	You are fully immersed in a virtual environment and cannot see or interact

	elements.	with the real world while using VR.
Example	Using a smartphone app that displays directions on your screen as you walk or a game like Pokémon GO where digital creatures appear in real-world locations.	Using a VR headset to enter a simulated world, such as a virtual tour of a historical site or a VR game that transports you to a different world.
Summary	AR adds to real world experience	VR replaces real world with a fully digital one

Importance of Augemnted reality and Virtual reality in teaching science

Augmented Reality (AR) and Virtual Reality (VR) can significantly enhance science education in various ways:

1. **Immersive Learning Experiences**: VR can transport students to different environments or time periods, such as exploring the solar system or ancient civilizations, providing a deeper understanding of concepts that are difficult to grasp through textbooks alone.

2. **Interactive Simulations**: Both AR and VR can create interactive simulations of complex scientific processes, such as chemical reactions or cellular functions, allowing students to visualize and manipulate variables in real time.

3. **Enhanced Engagement**: AR and VR can make learning more engaging by providing interactive and visually stimulating content. This can help capture students' interest and make difficult concepts more accessible.

4. **Safe Experimentation**: VR can simulate experiments and scenarios that might be hazardous or impractical in a traditional classroom setting, allowing students to explore and learn without risk.

5. **Personalized Learning**: AR and VR can be tailored to individual learning styles and needs, providing personalized educational experiences that can cater to different levels of understanding.

6. **Improved Spatial Understanding**: AR and VR can help students develop spatial reasoning skills by allowing them to manipulate 3D models of scientific phenomena, which is particularly useful in subjects like physics and biology.

7. **Global Collaboration**: These technologies can facilitate collaboration between students and educators across different locations, enabling them to work together on virtual projects and experiments.

8. **Visualizing Abstract Concepts**: Concepts that are abstract or not easily visible, such as atomic structures or gravitational fields, can be visualized in a more concrete manner through AR and VR, making them easier to understand.

Overall, AR and VR have the potential to make science education more dynamic, interactive, and effective by providing students with hands-on, immersive learning experiences.

Questions:

1. List differences between learner centred and teacher centred approaches.

2. What are the differences between learner centred and teacher centred approaches?

3. What are the important methods and approaches of teaching chemistry? Explain the significance of laboratory method and list out its merits and demerits.

4. What is the importance of Demonstration method in chemistry? List out the criteria of a good Demonstration.

5. What is the importance of demonstration method in chemistry? Listout the criteria of good demonstration.

6. Illustrate with example inductve and deductive approaches to teach chemistry? Mention their merits and limitations.

7. What are the methods and approaches of teaching Chemistry? Explain the inductive approach of teaching with an example. List out its merits and limitations.

8. Explain inductive and deductive approaches with chemistry example.

9. Explain inductive and deductive approaches with suitable example of chemistry teaching. List their merits.

10. Give example for Inductive & Deductive method

11. What are the differences between Inductive & Deductive method?

12. What is meant by project method? With the help of chemistry explain the steps of project method. What is the role of teacher in it?

13. Write four programme frames to the topic 'water'.

14. Write any three frames of linear programmed learning on the topic 'chlorine'

15. What is scientific method? Explain the steps involved in the scientific method.

16. Explain the steps of scientific method

17. How would you develop scientific attitude by teaching chemistry?

18. What is meant by project method? With the help of a chemistry explain the steps of project method. What is the role of teacher in it?

19. What are the points to be kept in mind to ensure the success of lecture cum demonstration method? Mention its merits.

20. What do you mean by laboratory method? Explain the steps and listout its merits and limitations.

21. IIow would you develop concepts in chemistry by using concept attainment model?

22. What is concept attainment model? Descrie its phases. Mention its merits.

23. What is augmented reality? What is its importance in teaching Chemistry?

24. What is virtual reality? What is its importance in teaching Chemistry?

25. What is the difference between augmented reality and virtual reality?

UNIT IV- Co-curricular activities of teaching Chemical science

4.1 Organization - Science Club, Science Museum, Science fairs, Science exhibitions

Science Club

Science Club is very essential in teaching science. How laboratories are important, in the same way science club also important. In science teaching process laboratory is considered as heart of science, curriculum where as science club is considered as the blood of it.

Some concepts cannot taught either in the classroom or in the laboratory, for such concepts science club provide better opportunities. It involves two major principles learning by doing and learning by living.

Meaning of Science Club:

The future of India belongs to youth and science. Therefore there should be a vast place for science club in the school curriculum.   *-According to Devis*

The club offer the pupil an opportunity for facilities which we do not have in the curriculum. The curriculum work is formal whereas the club activities are informal.

-According to Maclean

Aims of science club

1. To make proper use of leisure time

2. To develop individual and group initiative.

3. To create students interests in his every day experiences and his environment.

4. To develop scientific attitude among students and to inculcate a training in scientific method and to broaden his scientific outlook.

5. Provide the students with opportunity to develop his explorative creative and inventive faculties.

6. To develop a habit of co-operation in the students.

7. To encourage students participation in teaching learning process

8. To provide encouragement to club members for under taking some difficult, complicated and even risky experiments which are not permitted to be undertaken in regular class.

9. To allow opportunities to young students to learn practical applications of science.

10. To identify and nurture the would be scientists of country.

11. To familiarize the students with recent advances in science.

12. To exchange information with other science clubs.

Objectives of science club

- Providing opportunity to learn science independently.

- Learning science scientifically.

- Familiarization of students with problems and issue related to science.

- Involvement of students in activities.

- Stimulation to critical thinking.

- Science club provide non-formal atmosphere.

- Students can purse their interests and scientific hobbies.

- Science club as an outlet for talented students in science.

Activities of science club

1. Certain activities can be selected by the members of the club according to available resource.

2. Arranging science exhibitions, Film shows and science fairs.

3. Arranging science discussions, debate, essay writing, Guest lecturer etc.

4. Arranging the science excursions and visits.

5. Conducting workshops

6. Celebrating the science days, Scientists birthdays.

7. Collecting, Mounting and preserving the specimens.

Organization of science club

Most of the school houses are made like Mars, Jupiter, Mercury houses etc. science club on the name any scientist like Newton house, Einstein house etc.

1. The senior science teacher may be the Sponcer.

2. The principal/Headmaster of the school may be Patron

3. The resources of the school should be made available to the club.

4. An elective executive committee formed from the club members/students.

5. Executive committee: Chairman, Secretary, Joint Secretary, Treasurer, Librarian, Store keeper, Publicity in charge, Class representative.

6. A nominal membership fee should be charged from every member.

7. Other resources should be tapped by the club.

8. The members of the club should be encouraged to extend the activities of the club in their locality.

The duties of office bearers should be

1. **Patron:** To extended all the facilities to the club for its effective working.

2. **Spencer:** To look after, Guide, Lead.

3. **Chairperson:** To prescribe over the function of the club and over the meetings of the executive committee.

4. **Secretary:** To maintain the minutes of the meetings of the club.

5. **Join Secretary:** To assist the secretory.

6. **Treasurer:** To collect subscriptions and maintain the accounts.

7. **Librarian:** To issue and receive book, maintain catalogue.

8. **Store Keeper:** To keep record and equipment of the club

9. **Publicity in charge:** To publish the activities of the club in and outside the school.

Chairman: The selected representative of the student. He should preside over all the formal functions organized by the club.

Secretary: He / She is also an elected member. He is to look after and maintain a proper record of various activities of the club. He should call a meeting of the executive committee in consultation with the chairman and in accordance with the constitution of the club.

Treasurer: He / She is the person who is responsible for collection of subscription/membership fee for the club. He /She has also to maintain a proper accounts of receipts and expenditure of club.

Importance of science club

- Conducting a special day events in school.

- Organization of exhibition, science fairs etc.

- Developing awareness regarding science field.

- Developing the inventions attitude among learners.

Science Museum

A science museum is a type of museum that focuses on exhibiting scientific knowledge and innovations. They typically offer interactive exhibits, educational displays and hands-on activities related to various fields of science such as physics, biology, chemistry, astronomy, and technology. Science museums aim to make science accessible and engaging for people of all ages, often incorporating elements of fun and discovery to inspire curiosity and learning about the natural world and scientific principles.

Objectives of Science Museum

Science museums have several key objectives, including:

1. **Education:** To inform and educate visitors about scientific concepts, principles, and advancements in an engaging and interactive manner.

2. **Inspiration:** To inspire curiosity and a love for science by showcasing the wonders of the natural world, technological innovations, and historical scientific achievements.

3. **Public Engagement:** To foster a deeper understanding of science and its relevance to everyday life, encouraging public participation and discussion.

4. **Hands-On Learning:** To provide interactive exhibits and activities that allow visitors to explore scientific ideas and conduct experiments.

5. **Promotion of Scientific Literacy:** To help people of all ages understand and appreciate the role of science in solving global challenges and improving quality of life.

6. **Preservation and Research:** To collect, preserve, and research scientific artifacts, specimens, and historical materials for future generations.

7. **Community Involvement:** To serve as a community hub for science-related events, workshops, and educational programs.

Steps of organisation of science museum

1. **Define Vision and Mission**: Establish the goals and objectives of the museum. Determine what you want to achieve and how you want to impact your audience.

2. **Develop a Master Plan**: Create a detailed plan outlining the museum's layout, exhibits, and infrastructure. This includes space planning, design concepts, and visitor flow.

3. **Secure Funding**: Obtain financial support through grants, donations, sponsorships, and fundraising events. This is crucial for covering construction, exhibits, and operational costs.

4. **Design Exhibits**: Develop interactive and educational exhibits that align with the museum's mission. Collaborate

with scientists, educators, and exhibit designers to ensure content accuracy and engagement.

5. **Build Infrastructure**: Construct or renovate the physical space, including exhibit halls, educational areas, and visitor amenities. Ensure the building meets safety and accessibility standards.

6. **Acquire Collections**: Collect and curate scientific artifacts, specimens, and interactive displays. Ensure they are properly documented and preserved.

7. **Develop Educational Programs**: Create programs and workshops for various age groups and educational levels. This might include school field trips, public lectures, and hands-on activities.

8. **Recruit and Train Staff**: Hire knowledgeable staff and provide training on exhibit maintenance, visitor interaction, and educational programming.

9. **Market and Promote**: Develop a marketing strategy to attract visitors. Utilize social media, local media, and community outreach to raise awareness.

10. **Launch and Operate**: Open the museum to the public. Ensure smooth operations by regularly updating exhibits, maintaining facilities, and evaluating visitor feedback.

11. **Evaluate and Improve**: Continuously assess the museum's impact and performance. Gather feedback from visitors and staff to make improvements and adapt to new trends in science and education.

Importance of Science museum

Science museums play a crucial role in education and public engagement with science. Here are a few reasons why they are important:

1. **Educational Opportunities**: They provide hands-on learning experiences that can make complex scientific concepts more accessible and understandable, especially for students of all ages.

2. **Inspiration and Curiosity**: By showcasing the wonders of science and technology, they inspire curiosity and creativity, encouraging visitors to explore scientific fields and pursue careers in STEM (Science, Technology, Engineering, and Mathematics).

3. **Community Engagement**: Science museums often serve as community hubs, offering programs, workshops, and events that engage people from diverse backgrounds in science-related activities.

4. **Preservation and Interpretation**: They preserve scientific artifacts and offer interpretations that help the public understand the historical and contemporary significance of scientific discoveries and innovations.

5. **Interactive Learning**: Many science museums feature interactive exhibits that allow visitors to experiment and observe scientific principles in action, which can enhance learning and retention.

6. **Promoting Critical Thinking**: They encourage visitors to question, analyze, and think critically about scientific issues and current events, fostering a more informed and scientifically literate society.

Science fairs

A science fair provides an excellent opportunity for display and dissemination of various activities that are being carried over by the science club.

➤ A science fair can also serve the purpose of acquainting the parents in particular and people of locality in general with the diverse nature of scientific work that is undertaken in the school.

➤ In recent years government agencies encourages the organization of science fair.

- The encouragement provided in the form of financial and other help.

- Science fairs are encouraged by NCERT and SCERT of various states

Objectives for organizing the science fair

- To encourage the students to try out their ideas and to apply their knowledge of science into some creative channel.

- To provide opportunities to students to see for themselves some achievements of their colleagues and in this way stimulate them to plan their projects.

- To make science activities more popular among the students there by hoping to improve standards of performances.

- To encourage bright and enthusiastic students having special science talent.

- To identify the talented students in science and nurture the future scientists.

- To provide an opportunity to the people of area to come in contact with school and to meet the teacher and student.

- To provide a competitive forum to various science clubs in the area.

Organization of science fair

Before the Science Fair

To start organizing the science fair, you have to gather a group of people who will be responsible for the conceptualization and the implementation of the science fair. It could be a group of teachers, students, and researchers, among others.

- **Set Goals for the Science Fair:** The science fair should be celebrated for a reason. It is important that you set goals for the program. These are the objectives that you and your participants should achieve at the end of the fair. You have to make the experience positive for the participants. They should feel a sense of accomplishment. It is also your goal to give ample opportunity for students to showcase what they researched or developed.

- **Set the Date and Venue:** Find a location that can accommodate the number of participants that you expect and the materials that are needed in the fair, including chairs and display boards. You can always make use of your library, classroom, gym or cafeteria for the science fair to too many costs. In determining the date, avoid scheduling it on a day that is full of activities.

- **Create Interactive Activities:** Basically, one of the activities for the science fair is the showcasing of the students' investigatory and research projects. But apart from that, you can devise other fun and interactive activities such as science-inspired games. You can also invite prominent resource speakers to have a talk about biology or anything related to science.

- **Plan the Schedule:** Draft the schedule for the event. This will be needed for your invitation. Calculate the amount of time for each activity. Let us say the time dedicated to setting up the room will be at least six hours. So, the preparation should start the day before the fair. Judging should take 3 hours; visitation of booths shall be at least one hour, and so forth.

- **Recruit Staff and Volunteers:** You cannot do it alone. Of course, you have to ask the help of volunteers. The number of volunteers depends on the size of the event. The volunteers will help in the room setup, registration, ushering guests, monitoring the event and others.

- **Decide on Awards:** Consider if you want to acknowledge the participation of the students. You can create a customized certificate which will be distributed on the day of the fair. Determine the awards (first-place, second-place, third-place, minor awards, etc.) and create the criteria for judging.

- **Invite Visitors:** Promote your event through various strategies. You can post on your bulletin boards or announce it publicly. You can also use the power of social media to spread the science fair. Of course, to be formal, you can produce invitation cards. These will be given to special guests and judges. Include in your invitation the schedule, date and location, program, awards and other benefits.

During the Science Fair

After all the preparation you have made, it is time for the science fair!

- **Set up the Room:** Ask the volunteers and the school custodians to help you in setting up the room. Use your layout map to help direct those involved in the fair. Make sure that the stage and podium are presentable. Setup the tables, chairs, area for judges, display boards, research projects and everything that should be showcased in the fair.

- **Register Participants:** Record the attendance of the students and the participants. If they have submitted their projects for the fair, then give them a project code especially if judging has been blinded. Track any changes that may affect the fair, like students backing out of the fair. Direct the students and guests to the appropriate specific locations.

- **Orient Judges:** If the judges are complete, make sure that you orient them very well about the mechanics of the program and the criteria for judging. Ensure that the hold no bias in judging. Also, you can utilize blind judging to avoid favoritism.

- **Monitor the Fair:** The fair should start by now. The hosts shall have opened the science event and welcomed the guests. Now, you have to monitor the flow of the fair. Of course, it is normal that there are unexpected circumstances along the way. You have to manage it smoothly so as not to affect the fair. Always check if the students, judges, and guests are enjoying or doing well. Stick to your schedule to avoid inconsistencies.

- **Tabulate Scores:** After the ample time given for judging, tabulate the scores carefully. Total the score on each sheet file each score by category and collate score sheets. This is one of the most crucial stages. You have to be careful in tabulating the results as these will determine the winners. Create an official list of winners.

- **Distribute Certificates and Awards:** It is recommended that you conduct a small awarding ceremony on the last part of the science fair. It is a unique way of acknowledging the hard work and the brilliance of the students for their entries. Distribute certificate of participation for all students who attended. Also, acknowledge the presence of special guests and judges. Lastly, announce the major awards.

After the Science Fair

After the successful implementation of the science fair, the work still continues. There are certain things that you should do after the science fair.

Evaluate Your Program: Review if the goals and objectives of the program are being met. Assess how well you and your staff achieved in the fair. You can also send evaluation forms to the students who participated so that they can rate the science fair and provide feedback and suggestions for the improvement of the science fair.

Publicize the Fair: Lastly, you have to be proud of the science fair. Publicize the event in your school paper or in your official social media page. Include photos of the highlights of the science fair, winners, awards, etc.

Importance of science fair

- Science fairs which provides the opportunities to science students to share and learn new interests of students .the main importance's are :

- Science fair enables the students to display the outcome of their investigation.

- Help students to observe scientific projects, undertaken by other school .this helps to increase their knowledge sometimes students sense some scientific problem for future participation.

- Students get an opportunity to learn new techniques and methods.

- Helps to popularize science and science hobbies among students and community members.

- It helps to motivate towards science.

- Science fair contribute their social developments science fair increases the skill of presentation.

Science exhibitions

Science is a great blessing to mankind. Science exhibitions in schools play a pivotal role. Scientific exhibitions create a scientific spirit among the students, increasing thinking power and reasoning power. These can make the child creative and inquisitive. A child gets an opportunities to make a project or working model with own hands. These exhibitions can encourage a healthy competition in the student community.

Meaning of Exhibition

An exhibition is a public event at which pictures sculptures or other objects of interest are displayed for example at a museum or art gallery.

The public display of the things, objects, events, teaching learning aids and equipments, materials, resources, achievements and performance of the students related to teaching and learning of the subject science is known as Science Exhibition.

Objectives of Science exhibition

1. Promoting intrest in science and technology among younger generations.

2. Encouraging scientific and technological creativity among students and inculcating a sense of pride in their talent.

3. Encourage creativity among students.

4. To bring school into community and society.

5. To the future scientists to the limelight.

6. To know about the models, methods and techniques developed by teacher, students or institutions and to derive benefit from each other.

7. Encouraging problem solving approach and developing appropriate technologies, especially for rural areas and integrating and applying scientific ideas in daily life situations.

Organization of science exhibition

1. Set the goals of exhibition.

2. Set the date and venue.

3. Plan the schedule.

4. Register the participants.

5. Rules and regulations.

6. Different categories and sections should be marked for different types of displays by allotting separate places to them.

7. There should be proper arrangement of safety and security of the property of each participating team and also the total site of exhibition.

8. Awards and prizes should be given to the deserving participants and teams to provide necessary incentives and encouragement to them.

9. The host institution should try to appoint capable, honest and impartial judgment for these purposes.

Importance of Exhibition

1. Develop scientific attitude and critical thinking among the students.

2. Helps to develop the spirit of co-operativeness.

3. Application of scientific knowledge in new situations.

4. Develop the power of reasoning.

5. Improve the creativity of the student.

6. Facilitate the students to update their knowledge in science.

7. It gives chance for the students to speak well.

4.2 Activities- Excursions, field trips, visits, Puzzles

Excursions, field trips, visits

The traditional classroom, with its rows of desks and chalkboards, is evolving. In its place, the educational community is increasingly recognizing the myriad benefits of outdoor education and field trips. Venturing beyond the confines of school walls, students step into a world of experiential learning, where real-world experiences become powerful educational tools.

An educational excursion is a field trip to enhance a student's educational experience. It is usually conducted as part of a school program or curriculum and may last for a day or several days. The purpose of an educational excursion is to provide students with opportunities to learn about something new or different outside of the classroom setting.

Excursions can take many forms, but all should be carefully planned to maximise students' educational benefits. Some standard educational excursions include museum visits, historical site visits, play equipment venues, nature walks, plays, and observations of local businesses. Tours can also be combined with other activities, such as service projects, research projects, or hands-on learning experiences.

Types of field trips

1. Educational Tours: Visits to museums, galleries, or historical sites to enrich subject-specific knowledge.

2. Nature Trips: Expeditions to forests, parks, or beaches, promoting environmental awareness and scientific exploration.

3. Industry Visits: Tours of factories or businesses, offering insights into real-world applications of academic subjects.

4. Adventure Trips: Outdoor activities like camping or trekking, emphasizing teamwork, leadership, and survival skills.

Importance of field trip

Field trips are not merely outings; they are vital components of a comprehensive educational strategy. They bridge the gap between theoretical knowledge and its real-world application. By providing students with tangible experiences, field trips make learning more engaging, memorable, and relevant. Furthermore, they promote critical thinking, enhance observational skills, and nurture a sense of curiosity and wonder.

Field trips boost education by providing hands-on learning experiences that stimulate curiosity and engage students actively. They offer real-world applications of classroom lessons, improving deeper understanding and retention. Exposure to new environments, cultures, and ideas broadens students' perspectives and fosters critical thinking. Field trips promote social skills and teamwork as students interact with peers and teachers in different settings. These experiences can also create curiosity and motivation, making learning more interesting and enjoyable. By stepping outside the traditional classroom, students can connect theoretical knowledge to practical experiences, deepening their overall educational experience and cultivating a lifelong love of learning.

Organisation of field trip

1. Define Objectives: Clearly outline the educational goals and desired outcomes of the trip.

2. Choose a Destination: Select a location that aligns with the curriculum and offers relevant learning experiences.

3. Obtain Permissions: Ensure necessary permissions from school authorities, parents, and relevant authorities at the destination.

4. Prepare Students: Provide background information, safety guidelines, and expectations to students before the trip.

5. Arrange Transportation & Logistics: Coordinate transportation, accommodations (if required), and other logistical details.

6. Plan Activities: Design activities or guided tours that align with the educational objectives and engage students actively.

7. Ensure Safety Measures: Implement safety protocols, assign responsible chaperones, and conduct necessary risk assessments.

Benefits of field trips

1. Enhanced Learning Experience: Outdoor settings provide a dynamic backdrop for learning. Whether it's studying the ecology of a forest or the history etched in a monument, being physically present in the environment enriches understanding. Concepts learned outdoors often leave a lasting imprint, solidifying theoretical knowledge with tangible experiences.

2. Fostering Curiosity and Engagement: The great outdoors naturally ignites curiosity. Students, when exposed to unfamiliar terrains or novel experiences, are prompted to observe, question, and explore actively. This heightened engagement translates to a deeper connection with the subject matter, as the learning process becomes self-driven and exploratory.

3. Promoting Holistic Development: Outdoor education emphasizes holistic development. Activities such as team-building exercises, problem-solving challenges, and nature walks nurture not just cognitive skills but also emotional, social, and physical well-being. Students learn resilience, adaptability, and interpersonal skills in real-time, real-world scenarios.

4. Cultivating Environmental Stewardship: Direct interaction with nature fosters a profound appreciation for the environment. Field trips to parks, conservation areas, or wildlife sanctuaries instill values of conservation and sustainability. Students develop a sense of responsibility towards the environment, understanding their role as stewards of the planet.

5. Facilitating Experiential Learning: Outdoor education epitomizes experiential learning—learning by doing. Whether it's conducting experiments in a natural setting, navigating through challenging terrains, or studying biodiversity up close, students gain firsthand experiences that reinforce theoretical concepts and stimulate critical thinking.

6. Building Resilience and Confidence: Outdoor challenges, be it overcoming physical obstacles or adapting to unpredictable situations, build resilience. Students learn to step out of their comfort zones, confront challenges head-on, and emerge more confident in their abilities. These experiences instil a belief in one's potential, fostering a growth mind-set.

7. Cultivating Cultural Awareness and Empathy: Field trips often expose students to diverse cultures, traditions, and communities. Interacting with different socio-cultural environments broadens perspectives, fostering cultural awareness and empathy. Students develop a nuanced understanding of global issues, appreciating the richness of diversity and the interconnectedness of the world.

8. Inspiring Lifelong Learning: Perhaps one of the most enduring benefits of outdoor education is its potential to inspire lifelong learning. The transformative experiences, profound insights, and memorable moments encountered outdoors often kindle a lifelong passion for exploration, inquiry, and discovery. Students become lifelong learners, driven by curiosity and a thirst for knowledge.

Safety measures should teachers take while taking students for field trips:

Safety is paramount during field trips. Here are essential safety measures:

1. **Risk Assessment**: Identify potential hazards and develop strategies to mitigate risks.

2. **Chaperone Training**: Ensure chaperones are trained and aware of safety protocols.

3. **Emergency Plans**: Establish clear procedures for emergencies, including first aid, evacuation, and communication.

4. **Supervision**: Maintain appropriate student-to-chaperone ratios to ensure adequate supervision.

Post field trips duties

After the field trip, several post-trip activities ensure the experience's continuity and effectiveness:

1. **Debriefing Sessions:** Reflect on the trip, discuss experiences, and consolidate learning.

2. **Assessment**: Evaluate students' understanding through assignments, presentations, or discussions related to the trip.

3. **Feedback**: Collect feedback from students, chaperones, and other stakeholders to improve future trips.

4. **Documentation**: Document the trip with photos, videos, or journals, creating lasting memories and educational resources.

Puzzles

Puzzle a problem that may take many forms, including games and toys, and is solved through knowledge, ingenuity, or other skills. The solver of a puzzle must arrive at the correct answer, or answers, by thinking or putting pieces together in a logical way. There are different genres of puzzles, from word puzzles such as crosswords and number puzzles to mechanical puzzles such as the Rubik's Cube. Puzzles often serve as a method of keeping one's mind active and as a pastime, as seen by their prevalence in daily newspapers and online, but they are also at the centre of fiercely contested global competitions such as the World Puzzle Championship.

Puzzle types

- **Word Search:** Find hidden words in a grid of letters.

- **3D Puzzle:** Piece together intricate structures in three-dimensional glory.

- **Logic Grid Puzzles:** Think outside the box to solve complex scenarios with cunning clues.

- **Sudoku Puzzle:** Arrange numbers in a 9x9 grid, testing your numerical prowess.

- **Cryptic Crossword:** Unlock the secrets of cryptic clues and unveil the hidden answers.

- **Mechanical Puzzles:** Manipulate physical objects to unravel their hidden mechanisms.

- **Floor Puzzles:** Delight in giant puzzles that span the expanse of the floor, captivating both kids and adults alike.

- **Escape Rooms and Quality Puzzle Hunts:** Immerse yourself in interactive adventures that blend problem-solving and mystery-solving.

- **Picross Puzzles:** Decipher a grid of squares to reveal a hidden picture.

- **Animal Puzzles:** Delight the little ones with puzzles featuring their favorite furry friends.

Benefit of puzzles

- **Improve short-term memory:** Working on a puzzle reinforces connections between brain cells, improves mental speed and is an effective way to improve short-term memory.

- Enhance mood: Puzzles increase the production of dopamine, a chemical that regulates mood, memory, and concentration. Dopamine is released with every success as we solve the puzzle.

- **Make it easier to unwind:** Although it is tempting to unwind by watching the television or by reading on a tablet, the body should avoid screen time before bed. Puzzles provide a much better opportunity to relax, making it easier to fall asleep and properly switch off.

- **Improve visual and spatial reasoning:** You need to look at individual parts of a jigsaw puzzle, or available spaces in a crossword puzzle and figure out how to fit the pieces or words into their space. If done regularly, this will improve your visual and spatial reasoning skills.

- **Offer stress relief:** By doing a jigsaw puzzle, you are getting the same benefits as if you meditated. The stress of everyday life disappears and is replaced by a sense of peace and tranquillity that lowers your blood pressure and heart rate.

- **Sharpen logic and reasoning:** Puzzles are intended to exercise your brain. Crossword puzzles, riddles, word searches and logic problems can all activate different parts of your brain, helping you to hone your critical and analytical thinking skills.

4.3 Funny experiments of Chemistry- need and importance

Science experiments are a type of scientific investigation that seeks to answer a question through observation and experimentation. The term "scientific experiment" is used in a precise way in the scientific method, but it has also been used more generally to mean an activity performed to test a hypothesis about how two or more variables interact. There are many types of experiments: lab or field, true experiments, observational studies, and surveys.

Following are the different types of science experiments:

- **Lab Experiments:** The experiment is conducted in a lab setting, and the results are analysed by scientists.

- **Exploratory Science Experiments:** An exploratory science experiment tests out new ideas or theories about how things work. This type of experiment does not have to be repeated because it's just for testing purposes.

- **Practical Scientific Experiments:** Practical scientific experiments involve observing changes that occur when you manipulate variables (such as temperature). These types of experiments can also lead to innovation.

- **Fieldwork Science Experiments:** These types of projects take place outside the laboratory or classroom under natural conditions; they often require collecting data while tracking animals, plants, and other organisms over time. Fieldwork may include identifying different types of species on your hike from tree frogs with their distinctive mating crickets to the usual wildlife like raccoons.

Need and importance Funny experiments

- **Develops scientific vocabulary:** Science experiments help students develop scientific vocabulary and terminologies that they can use throughout their lives when discussing the latest news in science.

- **They Get to Learn about Different Concepts:** It is a fun way to teach children about concepts like gravity, inertia, and friction using real-life examples through hands-on activities.

- **Allows teachers to access the knowledge of students:** Experiments allow teachers to assess how well students grasped certain principles at home or school while also giving them feedback on what should be taught next time around without having to rely solely on tests as a measure of understanding content covered so far in class.

- **Provide an Opportunity for Learners:** They provide an opportunity for learners to experiment themselves which helps improve critical thinking skills by observing various outcomes with different variables set up within specific parameters.

- **Provides Chances to Design and Execute:** The opportunity to design and execute their own experiments also helps students develop a sense of ownership which in turn encourages them to take more responsibility for what they learn, as well as have fun trying things out on their own.

- **Provides Chances of Hands-On Experiences:** Experiments provide learners with hands-on experiences that are not found elsewhere than by doing specific tasks themselves rather than just passively absorbing information through reading or listening.

- **They are taught about engaging with action:** Students can become more engaged when learning is associated with action – whether it be tinkering around in the lab setting up variables and testing hypotheses so they can see how theories about matter work; manipulating materials to test their properties; or exploring the natural world by making observations.

- **Emphasises on Critical Thinking:** Science Experiments emphasize critical thinking skills, problem-solving techniques, communication skills, and higher-order thinking.

- **They Are Taught About Scientific Methods:** They teach students about the scientific method – how scientists work on questions in science using experiments with variables that can be controlled so as not to lead to false conclusions.

- **Provides Students with Life Long Achievements:** These hands-on experiences prepare students for life after graduation – whether that means a four-year university degree program, apprenticeship programs, trade schools, community colleges with technical degrees, etc

Questions:

1. What are the objectives of science fair and science exhibition? Explain them.
2. What are the objectives of science club? How do you organise it?

3. Explain the activities that organise in the school through science club?

4. What is Science Club? What are the objectives of science club? Explain any two activities organise under Science Club?

5. What is excursion? How to organise it?

6. What are the importance of organising excursion?

7. What is puzzle? What are types of it?

8. What is the importance of puzzles in teaching – learning chemistry?

9. What is funny experiment? What are the importance of it?

References:

- https://byjus.com/chemistry/
- https://www.toppr.com/guides/chemistry/some-basic-concepts-of-chemistry/importance-and-scope-of-chemistry/
- https://vajiramandravi.com/quest-upsc-notes/famous-chemistry-scientists-of-india/
- https://science-education-research.com/teaching-science/
- https://ncert.nic.in/pdf/focus-group/science.pdf
- https://ddceutkal.ac.in/Syllabus/MA_Education/Education_Paper_5_SCIENCE.pdf
- https://www.frontiersin.org/journals/psychology/articles/10.3389/fpsyg.2022.1037400/full